STANDING IN THE PINK CLOUDS

Linda Rizzo Marzano

NEW HARBOR PRESS

RAPID CITY, SD

Marzano/New HarborPress
1601 Mt. Rushmore Rd, Ste 3288
Rapid City, SD 57701
www.newharborpress.com

Ordering Information:
Quantity sales. Special discounts are available on quantity purchases by corporations, associations, and others. For details, contact the "Special Sales Department" at the address above.

Standing in the Pink Clouds/Linda Rizzo Marzano. -- 1st ed.
ISBN 978-1-63357-375-8

Cover photo by photographer Mark Corneliussen, Tucson, AZ

Dedicated to Natalie, Rene, and Curtis, with love, and to all who suffer because of the diseases of alcoholism, drug abuse, and mental illness.

"Have courage for the great sorrows of life, and patience for the small ones. And when you have laboriously accomplished your daily task, go to sleep in peace. God is awake."

—Victor Hugo

Preface

THIS IS THE MEMOIR of a woman who has faced life's demanding terms, but not without a quest for understanding.

A compelling read for anyone going through any of life's challenges, the author shares intimate memories, mysteries, and the poignant emotion she has experienced of both pain and joy.

The author invites the reader to journey along with her to witness her picture of God in her life.

Written in an engaging style, her own voice becomes a tool to an exploration of soul. Experience the human condition up close, and perhaps find your own understanding of God's love.

All persons named in this book have been changed to respect their anonymity.

LINDA RIZZO MARZANO

Acknowledgments

THANKS TO RENÉ EHLERS, Grace Eileen Dilts, John Blakely, Jan and Lance Cargill, Sydney Lipman, Dr. Linda Ehlers, Jolene English, Caralee Martin, Noel Morgridge, Nancy E. Turner, and Ruth Ann Carlson Nagy.

Thanks be to God, and Linda JB Herrick, and Don Booth, without them this book would not have been possible.

CHAPTER 1

IT IS A GRAY Chicago day as I sit on the stoop of the house we are renting. It is a big, ornate house and must have been built in the twenties or thirties. The rooms are spacious with towering ceilings and windows. The old landlady lives upstairs, and we live downstairs.

Staring up into the drab sky through the naked black branches of the winter trees, I see them. They are paisley in shape. They move all around—everywhere. It must be them, the polio germs. I turned to go inside. On the door is a sign scrawled in big red letters, "QUARANTINE Polio." I don't understand this big word quarantine. I only know that it keeps me from going to school.

Inside, the doctors stand around my baby brother who is lying on the couch. They are talking softly about his condition.

I will learn decades later from my mother that deep within them, the doctors experienced immense fear. They are frightened to go home to their families. Maybe they will carry the germs to the people they love.

Baby brother Dean is OK. The polio has left him, but with an arm that will never function and hardly grow. The germs did not find me.

That winter I experienced a storybook Christmas. A child's dream came true.

The doll in the department store window is mine to keep. I marvel at her porcelain skin and glistening blue eyes; long, blond curls; blushing cheeks; and painted dark pink lips. Her rosy dress is long, full, and lacy. Little pearls sit in her earlobes. She is mine. I will keep her on my bed forever.

I still have her today.

We will be moving soon. I am in the middle of learning to tell time. I am afraid the new school will not be teaching what I am learning. What if they are ahead of where I am now? Do they know about Dick and Jane and their dog Spot?

The unpaved roads ooze liquid mud, deep and sucking. Our car can get stuck. Here is our brand new little house. It is our home for the next ten years. It will be filled with growing pains and joyous occasions. Mom says we have over eighty kids on our block. All of our homes were purchased on the GI Bill, because all our fathers have served in the military. What adventures are in store! It is a good place to be.

I will dream about going back and buying that home to live in for a long time.

CHAPTER 2

WE GO TO SCHOOL, come home, and play hard. We have streets and sidewalks to roller skate and ride our bikes on now, and a place to build our forts. We have corners to play ball, and that's where I broke my nose. Papa says I am vain to think I should get it fixed.

We must be home by the time the streetlights come on or, "You're in trouble!" Once we were late and everybody's mom and dad were gathered together, waiting. They looked like a lynch mob. It was weird. As if anything was going to happen to us.

In the heat of summer vacation, we play Monopoly in one of the neighbor kid's basements. In the mornings I help Mom hang clothes on the line, then I go for a swim in our vinyl pool. Once it was so hot at night that Papa let me swim naked. I felt like a snake slithering through the water. I wanted to do it again, but Papa said I am too old.

Coming home from school is pretty much the same every day. The house is unlocked, the beds are unmade, the ash trays are overflowing, and dirty dishes are stacked in the sink.

I know Mom is somewhere in the neighborhood. Her car is parked in front of the house. The keys are there on top of the visor. She could be at any of the thirty houses on our street. I like it that way. I can put everything in order, giving special care to the glasses. I hate when I drink milk and get to the bottom of my glass and find a buildup of a milk ring! I realize my mother's heart is not in her housekeeping.

Sometimes I come home to find she has torn up every room in the house. "Cleaning things out," she would say. I hate the mess everywhere. It was then I realized I have two mommies, a good mommy and a mean mommy. If things were not as she thought they should be, I might find something I didn't put in its proper place burned up on the back porch. I hated her for that, and I would tell her so in letters I left on her chest of drawers.

Papa is never home. He has to work. On his two-week vacation every summer he goes to Canada to fish with the men and my brother. Girls are not allowed. The fish fry's in the back yard after the trips are worth it. There is nothing like a fresh walleye filet rolled in cornmeal and fried. But I still want to go with the men.

To this very day I still want to go fishing in Canada.

School is upsetting me now. It seems I am always in trouble, and I don't know what I am doing wrong. Someone is doing terrible things like writing malicious letters to teachers and signing my name. Or they write bad words on the girls' bathroom walls and sign my name. I feel so ashamed, and I didn't even write them. We never found out who wrote those awful words, but my mom says if the principal calls me to the office one more time, my dad is going to hire a handwriting specialist. He will look at those words and prove that I did not write them. My parents' support makes me feel good. *So there, bad person, whoever you are. My family will prove I didn't do those bad things.* But the kids in school will never know the truth.

I have the best adventures in my teen years. On Saturdays, my girlfriends and I go downtown to the Chicago Loop. We travel by bus, then the L train. Chicagoans call it the "L" because the track is elevated above the street. On the bus, I sit with my friends and pretend to have a convulsive fit. That always gets them roaring with laughter. The girls look forward to this part of our journey.

When we arrive downtown, we make our way to Navy Pier. There, thousands of men in white bell-bottom suits with long black ties and little round white caps flood the sidewalks. Sailors! They google at us, and we google right back. The inevitable would happen, and they would ask us to dinner and a movie. Once, a sailor bought me a white gardenia. It was so perfect that it didn't seem real. Its soft small petals were pure white, its leaves dark green and waxy. I will never forget the smell, definitely heavenly.

The gardenia will be my favorite flower forever.

As evening draws near, the sailors leave to go wherever sailors go, and we leave for home.

Boys have always been dear to my heart. I love a lot of them from afar, but I don't really know them. As I am growing older, I notice my attraction deepening. They make me feel something I have never felt before. The older boys, the ones who are very masculine, they do things to my thoughts, my emotions, the way my body feels—swoony I guess I might say. I want one but will not let one get to me because I just don't see a reason.

I love the music and the wild imaginings of this time of my life. I can do anything! School dances are bitchin'. We get all dolled up and wait for a guy to ask us to dance. The music is great. The new dances are a blast. We do the Twist, the Stomp, the Stroll, the Watusi, the Pony, the Mashed Potato and everything else we see on the American Bandstand TV show. We rat our hair, teasing it up as high as we can, then spray it up stiff. We line our eyes black, wear cotton-candy pink lipstick, and put on tight skirts and stacked heels. What a feeling. What a look.

Now, there are three kinds of kids in school. The Goodie Two-shoes, I am not. The jocks, I am not. The greasers, I am not. I am just kind of a blend of them all, I guess. I get along with any of them. This is best. The only things that make life miserable are Kotex, garter belts, and bras.

I watch over my baby brother. He is four years younger than I am. The kids can be mean to him, calling him "rubber arm" and "polio Joe." I hide in the bushes and jump out, raining down my holy terror upon them. After that, they leave him alone. My brother Dean loves his sissy—me.

Papa says we are getting out of Chicago, moving to Wisconsin. I won't be graduating with my friends.

CHAPTER 3

RELATIVES. WHAT A CONCOCTION.

Papa's side:

Christmas reunions took place in a huge rented hall with a blazing stone fireplace. Jillions of teens and kids horsed around all over the hall with "Rocking around the Christmas Tree" playing on the record player. We drew names for presents, and each of us took turns opening them. Later, the adults got a game of Rummy Royal going, but no one under sixteen was allowed to play. I never got to play. By the time I was sixteen, the Rummy-playing adults were slowly dying off.

I bought my own Rummy Royal board and, every Christmas, I try to get folks together to play with me.

Papa is the second youngest of ten—only one brother, the rest are girls. I think that is why he is so good to Mama. He knows women. Most of his sisters are crazier than hell—powerful, belligerent, and psychic. Only one is sweet to me, Aunt Betty. But I love Aunt Thelma most. She has an extra thumb. What a gas! Whenever she visits, the kids in my neighborhood line up for blocks to see her extra thumb. I should charge admission. I asked her once why she didn't have it removed. She said she would miss it. She uses it for everything.

One of Aunt Thelma's great-grandchildren was born with her extra thumb.

Grandpa, who was exiled from Italy, died when my father was a small boy. Grandpa was known as the Godfather in the Pennsylvania town where they lived. Papa says he would make a tea from the afterbirth and placenta for women who just had a baby. The only thing Papa remembers about his father is that when he died, they had more food in the house than ever before.

Papa was sick with chorea as a boy. When he walked, his skinny little legs would knock together and bleed at the ankles and knees. He couldn't even hold a pencil in his hand. If he tried to write, the pencil flew into the air.

Grandma, on the other hand, came from a well-to-do family. When Grandma was young, she rode in her own horse and buggy. She calls me "Missy" in a hissing tone.

Grandma died while I was in labor for my firstborn.

Uncle Jimmy, Aunt Thelma's husband, was the first funeral I ever went to. I had to beg to go because everyone said I was too young to view a dead body. It wasn't so bad.

Mama's side:

Mama's family are poor dirt farmers. Mama is somewhere in the older part of the group of nine kids who lived. I don't know how many babies Grandma lost.

Reunions for Mama's side are usually at one relative's farm or another. Millions of people show up at those reunions with some of the best eats you can imagine. There is always made-from-scratch cinnamon rolls, banana cream pie, baked chicken, and purple deviled eggs.

Grandma is short and stout. Grandpa thin and red. Red hair, red freckles, red face, and always a bottle of something in his right hand. He works hard, a crane operator, and drinks hard. He came home long enough to make another baby, I think.

Most reunions start out with Great-Aunt Minnie saying grace. The woman cries for ten minutes through each prayer. I always look at my cousins with my head bowed and snicker.

I found out in later years that Aunt Minnie lost all her brothers and sisters in the same week, two boys and two girls, to the great influenza epidemic.

When we stay at Grandma and Grandpa's farm, we are assured a feather bed. What a pleasure. There is always a chamber pot under Grandma's bed, even though the bathroom is only ten feet away.

I like to go out to gather the eggs first thing every morning. This I enjoy beyond belief. I don't know why, because I must constantly dodge attacking roosters and geese. Those are the meanest critters on earth. Why they pick on me, I'll never know. Grandma is very good with the ax. I learned firsthand where the saying "running around like a chicken with its head cut off" came from. Grandma lets me churn the butter too.

One winter, Grandma told me that one of the dogs had puppies up in the hay loft in the barn and I could go find them. What a cruel thing to do. I will never forget it. I climbed up into the loft with great anticipation, only to find dead puppies riddled with worms. Why did she tell me about the puppies? Didn't she have sense enough to know they died of the cold?

I will be cremated when I die.

On one visit to the farm, I shared a bed with my Aunt Verna. She is only four years older than me. Can you believe that? She told me to pull the covers all the way to the end of that big brass bed to get rid of the bed bugs before we got in. I was sure she was kidding or just trying to scare me. But we pulled the covers to the end of that bed and sure enough, black beetle-like bugs scurried down the sheets and off somewhere before we crawled in. I don't know how, but we slept fine.

To this day I don't want to hear "sleep tight and don't let the bed bugs bite!"

I have never seen people cry or laugh harder in all of my life as when I am with Mama's family.

Grandma's and Grandpa's farm will be in my memory forever. No loving touches, but indelible just the same.

• CHAPTER 4 •

THE MOVERS ARE HERE, and Mama hasn't even cleared out the refrigerator. They just carried it out of the kitchen with everything in it. We will be in our new home in Wisconsin in a few hours. It's just north of Milwaukee. Home for a while will be the upstairs apartment of a very old house.

The first evening, I went outside and found the cold penetrating. I looked up to the sky and nearly lost my breath. What an amazing sight it was. I had never seen anything like it. Our home in the suburbs of Chicago was so close to Gary, Indiana, and the fiery smoke stacks of the steel mills blackened the sky day and night. I knew only God could create the miracle I saw in that sky. A black velvet canvas studded with stars I never knew existed. Stars bright and twinkling in colors of blue, yellow, and red. I want to write to my friends back in Chicago and tell them about this Wisconsin sky, but I could never describe its magnitude.

It is so dark at night in the apartment that when I get up to use the bathroom I am not sure whether my eyes are open or closed. I know now what it must be like to be blind.

Our new town is small: one grocery store, one bank, one hardware store, a church on each end, and half a dozen taverns in between. The lakeshore is walking distance from everywhere.

Dairy farming is the deal here. You can't buy margarine anywhere. There are several small cheese factories where we can go anytime and taste all the different cheeses. Some melt in my mouth and taste delicious. Others taste just as bad as they smell. Who would eat that stuff?

My first day of school is a shocker. I came from a class of a thousand seniors to a class of maybe twenty. There is a queer smell in the halls everywhere—like shit! If looks can kill, I am dead. My new classmates are farm kids. They have been up since five o'clock in the morning doing chores before school and are dressed accordingly. In I walk with my ratted hair, black-lined eyes, pink lips, tight skirt, and stacked heels looking for the nearest place to catch a smoke.

It is some months down the road now, and the shock has worn off for both my classmates and me. I am starting to appreciate where I am. I've made a few friends and drunk a lot of beer. Everyone drinks beer here. It's only a dime a glass. In Chicago, my friends and I talked about sex and what it might be like, but these farm kids are doing it anywhere. I can hardly believe it.

I got a firsthand experience with dairy farming from a boy in my class. One Saturday he invited me to visit his family's farm and he showed me around. The barn where all the cows were milked was an eye-opener for me. When we entered the barn, ammonia from the cow's urine burned my nose and eyes. I could barely catch a breath. Then there was the manure—heavy piles, the consistency of batter. The smell was horrific. I could actually taste it in my mouth. All thoughts of ever being a farmer's wife ended right there in that barn.

Summer came and Papa and Mama bought a cabin on the lake. It has a huge glassed-in porch with a fireplace. That's where I live most of the time. I wake to deer feeding on the lawn in the morning and us going water skiing in the afternoon. The bugs are vicious, especially the mosquitoes.

One night after a date, I told the fellow to drop me off at the top of the lane that leads down to our cabin and I would walk home.

What a mistake that was. Swarms of mosquitoes attacked me. To defend myself, I took off my wrap-around skirt and whirled it madly as I headed for cover.

Fall has arrived. Papa has sent me off to college for one year to get my M.R.S. degree. He says that this will be a good place to meet a man and that I don't need a full education because I will just be a housewife with children anyway.

I never want to say my father was wrong about anything, but by God, my daughter will graduate from college if I have to drag her there every day.

Surprisingly, college agrees with me. I am getting good grades and have had a keen awakening, a thirst for knowledge. I am making good use of the time I am here and wonder how I might find a way to go the whole four years.

One afternoon I was in the Student Union and noticed an announcement about a film that would be shown for the girls on campus about venereal disease. Some of the girls who went the first night told us there were naked men in the film. Word spread like wildfire. The next night the lines were so long to see "Venereal Disease and You" that they had to show the film for three more nights. None of us had seen a naked man!

Another evening, while we were studying in the dorm, my roommate and I heard a loud thunder of voices outside. We flew to our window and saw hundreds of male students marching around shouting, "We want pants; we want pants." That sent a chill down my spine, followed by an explosion of excitement. Next came the public address system announcement. We were to shut our drapes and stay away from the windows. By that time, we were throwing every pair of panties we could spare right out our windows. It was mass hysteria. We laughed so hard we cried.

Well as things go, I met a nice man, Bill. He was a senior and lived close to my town. We hit it off and went together for two years. I loved him, and before we knew it, I was pregnant. We were married and headed for New Jersey where Bill had been recruited for work.

DRIVING OUT TO NEW Jersey was our honeymoon.

As we travel in our '57 Chevy, with a radio that only works when you bang on the dashboard, I notice all the signs for lobster. I've never had lobster. I want some lobster, but Bill says we are on a budget now and lobster is not on the menu. I am beginning to see a side to this man that I never had before.

His belt got tighter and tighter every year. I will live with this for the next eighteen years.

My precious, beautiful, petite baby girl, Yvette, was born in August of 1967. Life as I knew it before now never existed. It seems I have switched gears. I am in another world. I love taking care of her. She is not an ounce of trouble. She is a part of life I never knew could be reality.

Yvette and I sell Avon together every day. I put her in the neighbor's borrowed pram and we walk the neighborhood. The homes in my neighborhood are huge, old, and well-kept. I have never seen such character and charm. Signs hang here and there that say, "Make Love, Not War." It is a time when hippies roam the land. I think it's interesting, but time with my baby is all I live for.

I cry every night during the ten o'clock news. I see the names listed of our boys killed in Vietnam. Many of them are friends and past loves. It hurts. My baby brother Dean, now out of college and living the hippie lifestyle, tried to enlist in the army. He was rejected of course because of the polio. He still tried. God bless him.

New Jersey is not going to cut it for these Midwestern folks. We begin to feel the need to be closer to family and home, so Bill found a job in St. Paul, Minnesota.

My sweet baby boy, Kirk, was born in St. Paul, in May of 1969. His birth was difficult, as if he did not want to be born. My labor stopped when I reached the delivery room. It was a Catholic hospital, and the nuns urged me to "push, push, push!"

The day after he was born, Kirk was circumcised, and I was required to be there to watch. The experience was horrifying. The doctor cut his little foreskin, and blood rushed onto the table. I asked God why I had made the decision to have this done. No one told me what it would be like. I could not wait to hold and console him in my arms.

My mother came by train from Wisconsin to help with the household chores and take care of Yvette while I was in the hospital. As long as I live, I will never forget the reception Kirk and I received from his big sister when we came home from the hospital. We entered our apartment and she greeted us by lifting her dress and showing her little silk panties. Grandma had had success with the potty training! Yvette then kissed her new little brother and told him she loved him.

What a gracious time God has given me. A new window to my heart and soul has opened now because of my children. These little gifts have altered every way I think, feel, and live. They complete me. I did not know how much I was missing until they came into my life.

I am standing in the pink clouds of God's blessings.

Mama returned home after ten days of her greatly appreciated help and prepared to move back to Indiana where our lives began.

Papa will take a medical technology teaching job at the school he had attended as a young man. Once again, they will be in the thick of all the relatives. Brother Dean is having a lot of mental problems and will stay with them.

Mama called. Papa has cancer. I'm going home.

God, how he suffers.

No human being should ever suffer the way he does. *What is the matter with these doctors? Give him something to kill the pain. Please.*

To see and touch someone you love, lying in a coffin, feels like a plug has been pulled from your heart, draining your life force. *I miss you, Papa. I wish we could have had more time. I will make sure Mama is all right.*

I will miss Papa for the rest of my life.

Bill works long hours and is not around much. I have taken a janitorial job here in our apartment building that is allowing us to save for a down payment to purchase our first home. A washer, dryer, and a second car are in the future. We are finding Minnesota's winters brutal and the summers much too short.

One night Bill came home late because his car was stuck in the snow. His ears were nearly frostbitten. We decided it was time to find a place we could love, to live for the rest of our lives. We should move while the kids are still little. I did the research and came up with Tucson, Arizona.

CHAPTER 6

IT IS THE BEGINNING of the full force of winter, and we are on the road to Arizona. Bill is driving the rented moving truck, and I am taking the kids, the dogs, our luggage, and the TV in the station wagon. For days we drive, slip sliding all the way.

About the third day of the trip, we reached New Mexico and stopped for dinner. In this restaurant, I experienced an entirely new culture about which I knew nothing. Huge plates of colorful food—refried beans, rice, tacos, enchiladas, and burritos—were being carried to each table. The smell of the food was new to me and made me eager to try all of these new delights. From this first encounter, Mexican food became a part of our life from then on.

As we approached Tucson, with "Feliz Navidad" playing on the radio, it looks as if the city is under construction. There are trees that are completely green. The trunks, the branches, everything is bright green. These trees look soft with feather-like leaves. Huge saguaro cactuses tower majestically along the road. The giants with outstretched arms are strange to see for the first time. Until now, these cactuses were something I had only seen in a cowboy movie. This foreign, new land, the Sonoran Desert, has a beauty all of its own. I expected miles of sand and an oasis of palm trees. We experience joy in all we see.

We have rented an apartment across the street from an orange grove for six months. In the spring, the aroma of the grove engulfs our building with a sweet heavenly smell. We plan to grow our own oranges and gardenias when the tract home we bought is finished. The kids are back in school and adjusting quickly.

Our brand new house was finished in April. We moved in and felt right at home. Home for the next ten years.

Just as I always wanted to go back to Chicago and purchase my childhood home, so would my adult children long to purchase their childhood home.

The neighborhood houses are all on one-acre parcels and zoned horse property. It is a great place to raise the kids. Plenty of good neighbors and room to roam. We soon discover that the cries in the night are howling, screaming coyotes! They run in packs at night, and small dogs and cats are daily casualties. We found this out for ourselves, firsthand.

We decided to put a swimming pool in as soon as possible for the long, hot summers. The kids became champion swimmers and divers. There were many parties and wonderful times around that swimming pool.

Kirk bought a secondhand go-cart and spends every waking hour getting it to work. He asked permission from all the neighbors to drive the go-cart on the easement between the homes in the neighborhood. There were no objections, and Kirk is having the time of his life. Yvette has friends over to play Barbie dolls regularly.

Our days are filled with Cub Scouts, Girl Scouts, Little League, gymnastics, and church. Watching the children grow is wonderful. A time for fun, a time for love, and a time for challenges.

I lie in bed after my prayers and tell God I have never been happier in my life. "Please God, you can take all of this from me, but please protect my children. I will give up all I have, just take good care of my children."

God's caring, protecting, pink clouds surround our lives.

Being close in age, Yvette and Kirk fight a lot, but they have a special relationship too. Yvette is doing great in school. We found that Kirk was born with a learning disability called dyslexia. We deal with this problem on a daily basis, but we are progressing. Even his teachers are learning that he needs special attention and no longer put his desk in the hall as punishment for his deficit.

We never go anywhere. We have lots of visitors from cold country, but we are fine.

Mama called. Dean is in San Diego. It seems he took some bad drugs. He jumped off the Washington Street Bridge into the traffic below. He shattered his pelvis. He is alive. He is in the hospital. I must go to my brother.

The flight is only an hour from Tucson. I collect my bag, find my way out of the airport, and hail a cab. I discover a place rich with greenery and warm, moist air. My cab ride to the hospital reveals views of bright, sparkling blue ocean with little boats of all kinds, and palm trees. *God, what a beautiful place to be.* What it must be like to live here! No wonder my longhaired hippie brother made his way here for the winter.

At the hospital, I find my brother in good spirits and healing. He will be all right. He is glad to see me, and I give him a small radio with ear plugs to help him pass the time. It will be a while before he can go home.

Dean had visited us in Tucson a few months earlier, and it was then I realized how mentally handicapped he had become. I took him to a doctor and was told there is no help for him. He is disabled and later will be diagnosed paranoid schizophrenic.

I tried to find a way to keep Dean with me. We wanted to find him some kind of work for the handicapped. He could live with us. *God, help me help my brother.* He only stayed a few weeks. He was eager to see San Diego. He lived off the land, so to speak, until he had a bad trip. That is when he jumped off the bridge. Mama is flying out to take him home to Indiana.

Dean will be in State Care for the rest of his life. He will lose the use of his kidneys. He will be on dialysis as long as he lives. I will not be able to see my baby brother much for the rest of my life. He will not marry. He will not have children. I will never be an aunt. I will never visit him at his home. He is unable to write me. A part of my heart is broken. I pray for him unceasingly.

Life zooms by, and suddenly we have two teenagers. No one ever gave me a manual on how to raise teens, but I think we are doing well. Kirk is fourteen and becoming very defiant. He now has a rage problem, almost overnight.

There was a group from the local hospital speaking at the kid's high school on drugs and alcohol rehabilitation. I went. What they described fit Kirk to a T. How had I missed this? How could my son be involved in drugs and alcohol? I am petrified! We tried an intervention to get him help. He would have nothing to do with an intervention. He tells us he does not have a problem.

It is not long before everything starts to whirl out of control with Kirk. He ends up at juvenile detention. We are advised to leave him there until he agrees to go to rehab. For three days and nights he refuses help, and for the first time in my life, my guts are on the kitchen floor. My son is in trouble. We must help him. Rehab is the answer. Finally, he agrees to go.

I visit Kirk every day that is allowed. I miss him so much I could die. All my concentration is on solving his problem. I am in the center of a storm that is battering my heart.

Kirk went the whole nine yards in rehab and came home. We went on with our lives.

I have been working in real estate and saved a good amount of money. I want Bill to agree to our first real family vacation. I want to go to San Diego. Pacific Beach. We could rent a cottage on the seashore and take the kids to Disneyland before they are any older. Yvette is sixteen now, and Kirk is fifteen. Bill's answer is the usual, "No!" and, "We can't afford this." For the first time in our marriage, I demanded a "yes." I felt we really needed this time together as a family.

The six hours it took to get to California seemed like forever. The trip was exciting and our arrival exhilarating. One evening we saw the Olympic Torch being passed right on the street where we stayed. Disneyland was one funtastic moment after another. The cottage we rented on the beach was pure heaven. The ocean glistened in the afternoon sun. We rushed out to the waves and they spilled over us. It was thrilling. There was roller skating, boogie boards for surfing, bonfires at night, and sights we could hardly believe. There were some very unusual people around too. It was the best thing we ever did together as a family.

The morning after we arrived back home from our vacation, while the kids were still asleep, Bill said he wanted to talk to me. He seemed very nervous. He had been arrested for a lewd act and would have to serve jail time.

"What?" I demanded.

He repeated the information. And again, "What?" came from my mouth.

"What is a lewd act?"

He told me he had been arrested for soliciting a prostitute.

"No, this is not possible! How can this be?"

He interrupted with the fact that he would start his jail time the next morning. I told him he needed to see an attorney. He said he already had. The sentence is mandatory. Well then, I needed to see his attorney. This is ridiculous.

Bill arranged a meeting for me the following week. I drove downtown to the attorney's office and was greeted by a middle-aged man who called me into his office. He explained that Bill had been one of the unfortunate victims of a sting operation set up by the moral majority of Tucson to clean up Miracle Mile. He had an audio-tape and film of Bill's arrest and would allow me to hear and see it with Bill's permission. He phoned Bill, who gave permission for me to view his exploitation. The film was never produced, the attorney could not find it, but the audio tape of the incident was available.

I listened and could not believe my ears. Bill was having a great time and bargaining for price! Where the hell did he get money for a prostitute, let alone a lawyer?

We went to marriage counseling for the next six months at our pastor's recommendation. At the end of the sessions, the counselor asked what I wanted to do.

Without hesitation I said, "I want a divorce."

We had been married a long time, but I felt that Bill lived in his own world. He was hard-pressed to have any kind of conversation with any of us about anything. He did not interact with the kids, and I would say we just never understood him. We just accepted his ways. But I could not live like this anymore. Even in the counseling sessions he hardly spoke.

Bill moved out, took a job in California, and the kids and I tried to adjust. I went through a tough time feeling rejected, frightened, sad, and the kids did too.

We shared a divorce lawyer, at the advice of our pastor, and split everything down the middle. I got the kids. The following year showed me just what a turd Bill could really be. He balked at the fact that he would have to pay child support until the kids were eighteen.

We sold the house, and the kids and I rented a little townhome within walking distance of their high school. The first year on our own, my car died. My share of the divorce money was dwindling fast. If it wasn't one thing, it was another. At that point I thought every woman should divorce her husband to see what he is really like. Divorce brought out a side of Bill I never would have dreamed existed. And I was amazed that I did not miss him. How can you be together all that time and not miss the man you married? I realized that most of our married life, Bill worked and watched football. That was it. Nothing more, nothing less. He never said, "I love you."

The kids and I remained close and active in each other's lives.

CHAPTER 7

IT WAS NOT LONG before the single women in my neighborhood told me it was about time I got out. They knew the places to go. Places to meet men. So I went. The kids are old enough to take care of themselves.

The girls took me to Smuggler's Inn. It was clear across town, and I did not expect much of the evening. As we sat at our table, I had my eye on one fellow. He was tall and good looking, like my dad. I really hoped he would ask me to dance, but it really didn't matter because the girls and I were having a good time.

A short, muscular man with a mustache approached me and asked me to dance. I told him no thank you. I was busy talking with my friends. As he walked away, I wished I would have said yes. He came by later and offered to buy me a drink. I accepted. We danced. He held me close. He felt powerful, strong, and had a very masculine look about him. We danced every dance for the rest of the night. I was infatuated. I wanted to know more about this man. I wrote down his phone number at the end of the evening and told him I would call him. I felt a bit of trepidation about giving him my phone number.

By the time I got to the car with my friends, he was all I could think of and talk about. The girls warned me to be careful. He gave me a kiss before we parted, and my lips felt warm and tender.

Weeks went by, and busy as I was as a single mom, I could not wait to hear his voice. I finally called. He was getting ready to take his three-year-old son to the circus. *How sweet*, I thought. He wanted my number to call me back sometime.

LINDA RIZZO MARZANO

One day he called me back. His voice was deep and smooth. To this day, I have never heard a man with a voice that compared to his. It sent shivers down my whole body. We set a date. He would pick me up and we would go to dinner.

It has been a long time since I have been on a date, and finding what to wear and how to fix my hair is exacerbating. When I peer in the mirror to put on my makeup, I cannot help but see the toll divorce and trying to support two teens has taken on my face. It appears my flesh is hanging now. The old sparkle of my youth has passed. Somehow I will get going and pull this off. It is just a date.

I cannot remember all we talked about or what I ate. I was just overwhelmed with this charismatic, magical man who stirred yearnings in me I never knew I had.

From those moments, it snowballs. It is as if a new part of my soul is allowed to experience love, passion, and overpowering emotion. I love this man. The more I am with him, the more I know this is love. The more he attends to me, the more I am whirling. I think of him always. I never dreamed a man like him existed, except maybe in some romantic novel. I have stumbled onto one of the most unbelievable people in the entire world, and his name is Bert.

He loves me. No one has ever treasured me as he does. To think some people have had this experience all their lives. God, what I was missing! And my children love him too.

Within two years, we are married.

Yvette has moved out and is putting herself through college. What a feat! Kirk lives with us. We have tried to get Kirk to think about a trade school or something for after he graduates high school so he will be happy in the long run, but he flat-out refuses. He tells me, "I can take care of myself." I am unable to persuade him to find a trade that will make him happy in life.

Tony, Bert's son, is now five years old. He was given to us to care for the day we got back from our honeymoon in Puerto Vallarta, Mexico.

There are so many things about Bert that are wonderful. He is emotional, physical, intelligent, hardworking, and loving. He is the best father any child could have. It is impossible to list all the attributes he possesses. It would take me a lifetime. And he is my biggest fan!

During the twelve years we spend together, there are tremendous challenges in being a stepmother and living the blended family lifestyle. There are also many heartfelt times that Bert and I will share.

The fulfillment of Bert's and my relationship will sustain me the rest of my life.

Every holiday, our children and relatives experience the most fulfilling days at our home. Bert spares no expense. He works in the automobile industry in car sales. He told me to take care of the finances and just tell him how much money to make. There are summer vacations in a cabin on Mount Lemmon, trips to Hawaii and Las Vegas, and backyard barbecues.

On one trip to Hawaii, we went to the island of Kauai. We stayed at the Coco Palms where Elvis made his movie *Blue Hawaii*. Bert surfed at Nurses Beach where the movie *South Pacific* was shot. He gave no heed to the warning signs of a strong undertow; he had swum the New Jersey coast during hurricanes.

We found a place where shells were abundant. We both love shells. Shells of all varieties. We wanted to gather them all. Bert found a ledge under the ocean shore that provided a gold mine of shells. He would dive in and come up with handfuls, mouthfuls, of all kinds of precious shells. He would then walk toward me, handing me shells with his hands; then as if giving birth, he would protrude one shell at a time from his mouth. I exploded with laughter and amazement. He is such a character.

We had our try at snorkeling too. We decided everyone in the world should try snorkeling before they die. There is a whole other world within a world in the ocean. He made a doughball by rolling some bread in between his hands and threw it in the crystal blue water near me. It made all the fish swim toward me. How could God create so many different kinds of gorgeous fish? The colors were astonishing. At night, we went to our room to admire our day's collection of shells and drink the delicious mai tais Bert had learned to make from the fresh island fruit.

Bert collected rocks that were said to be from Peli, the volcano goddess. There were warnings posted around the island that said not to take the rocks of Peli or bad luck would follow. I could not reach the side of Bert that was superstitious. He brought the rocks home to Tucson.

The times I treasure most are the times we have alone. It is our little world. Our conversation never lags. There is always love emanating between us. He always holds my hand, if we are walking, sitting, or driving. We know we will be the happiest old couple in the world when that time comes.

Grateful and overflowing contentment fills my life each day because of Bert. Every night when he comes home from work and I hear the garage door go up, a part of me always leaps for joy. Then when he walks in the door, the sight of each other makes us both beam. We always embrace and kiss.

We danced through the pink clouds with God's love.

Sometimes I want time to stand still so that we might be able to just look at each other and touch each other for eternity. It seems I can never get enough of him.

I tell myself that I feel sorry for women who may only know about his kind of lovemaking in a romantic novel. I have the real thing right here.

One afternoon, he came home early. He wanted me to take a nap with him. I recall just looking at him lying on our bed the whole time. He was so handsome. His broad, bold face rested with his eyes closed. Large boned and very muscular, he had more hair on his chest than ten men, and I loved to bury my face into it. My eyes could not look at anything else. Most of the time we slept together like spoons in a drawer. Outside our window, a bird was singing as a bird never sang before. He sang for a long while. Whatever kind of bird he was, I didn't know, but we had never heard a bird sing such a beautiful song. Bert and I looked at each other, not speaking, listening to that bird's concerto.

Yvette has graduated from college now with a teaching degree. It was the proudest day of my life. She is a beautiful, bright girl and has the world before her. She married, but divorced after three years.

Years later I will find out from Kirk and Yvette about the physical abuse Yvette had to endure in her marriage.

Now Yvette is leaving us to live in San Diego, California. This was not in my plans. How will life be not having her drop in for the day? We have grown to be best friends.

Kirk has been living on his own for a long time. He comes by often and is a pure joy to see and talk to. I sense that he still battles his alcohol and drug addictions. How can I help him? When he leaves, he hides canned food from our cupboard in his clothes. My God, he does not have money for food? I have been attending Al-Anon for years now and have learned to mind my own business. He is a grown man. Whatever problems he is having are problems only he can solve. I pray for him. I know God will guide him.

Tony, Bert's son, has grown to be a good-sized teenager. He will have to play football. He has all the right stuff to play; plus, as in all the men in my life, he is an avid fan of the game. Tony and I have still not completely bonded as a mother and son would. What am I expecting? He has a mother.

Tony and I will be good friends the rest of our lives.

Bert wants to go to San Diego for a family vacation. We will stay with Yvette for a while. She met a man and fell in love. She is now pregnant. They haven't gotten married, but I'm excited. I am going to be a grandmother.

Kirk, Tony, Bert, and I made good time driving to California. We hardly stopped at all. I had packed finger foods to eat along the way. As we hit San Diego, our sports vehicle seemed to have a mind of its own and headed straight for the beach. It was mid-afternoon and the sun shone brightly over the entire ocean. Its sparkle was magnificent. The breeze was cool and smelled of fresh, salt air. We dropped our shoes and ran from the car to the bubbling, surging, cold waves as we hit the beach. It felt so refreshing after our long ride, and this was a perfect day. Thank you, God.

We stayed at Yvette's and her boyfriend's house a few days, then rented a motel room right on the beach. There were endless fun things to do and plenty of places to eat every kind of food we wanted. Days were spent at the beach. At night, we walked along the piers and boardwalks. Bert said this brought him back to the days when he was a kid in New Jersey. He wants to move here when Tony graduates from high school. At night, I found myself going to bed before the boys. They could not tear themselves away from the constant invitation of the ocean and all the things that our vacation beckoned to them.

When we returned to Tucson, Bert decided he wanted to get into better shape. One afternoon he was in the garage lifting with Tony's weight training set and noticed a lot of pain in his left arm. He called it quits.

That arm is bothering him on a continual basis now. He will go to the doctor. The doctor will find nothing wrong with him.

Christmas has come to our home again. As usual, Bert will make sure it is the best Christmas ever. From the tree to the presents, he wants us to have it all. Of course, all of our family will be here. Bert's father has been visiting us in the winter sometimes, and my mother has retired here in Tucson. Kirk will be by, and Yvette is flying in from San Diego with a very round, kicking stomach. She is a full bloom mother-to-be. Oh my God. I cannot wait for my grandchild to be born. I plan to go out to San Diego when she has the baby and stay with her a while.

Christmas was indeed a fabulous day. Everyone took their turn with the new video camera. Good food, good people, good times. Thank you, God; thank you.

Bert is not feeling well enough to go to work. This man, who never took any time off except for Little League, is not feeling good. His arm is killing him, and I am about to make some demands on the doctors who cannot find anything wrong. We even had one doctor tell me that my husband has a "head problem." My husband does not have a head problem!

Finally, we got a referral to a doctor to look at his arm. He ordered an X-ray. Well hello! We have been screaming for an X-ray for months. The doctor wants us to meet him in his office for the results soon.

Bert and I arrived at the doctor's office and found ourselves being ushered into the doctor's conference area. He came in, pulled out the X-ray, and said that the humerus of his left arm was nearly gone. He was sorry to tell us that Bert has cancer. A spike of adrenaline filled my body. The world stopped and went into slow motion at the news.

We must have conferred about all our options and what we could do for an hour when Bert asked, "How long can I live?" He is forty-three and asking how long can he live!

The doctor replied, "Two months to two years."

Bert said that he wanted the two years, and we need to start now to make that happen. We were sent to a hospital for a MRI or CAT scan. It is all a blur to me. This is the beginning of someone else's life. It cannot be happening to us. For endless days we ran from one kind of doctor to another, dealing with rising pain that turned to torture for the next few months.

Bert's father flew in to help. We finally reached the stage of what they call "pain management," with the help of our hot tub, which Bert uses every evening. The cancer has metastasized, and my darling husband has tumors everywhere you can fit one in his body. One in particular really disturbed Bert, when his eye starting protruding. The tumor behind his eye was pushing his eyeball out. With mass radiation and chemotherapy, the tumors seemed to be restrained from their gruesome destruction. Thank God.

He is now being fed through a tube in his chest. Through this terror, my love for him gives me the strength to take care of him. I get into the shower with him to cleanse his pain-filled body. I cook, wash, and do all the things anyone would do for someone they adore. I love being his right-hand gal. No one but me is allowed to take his left arm out of its sling because I am the one who does it the best.

The time we share watching TV, listening to music, and reading are the most blessed days. I treasure every moment we have. I know our time is short. Please God, either take him soon so he does not suffer or make him well now!

Bert has been in the hospital two times. We bring him home and take good care of him. Someone said something about hospice and we said, "No, we are going home."

Yvette called. She is in the hospital. She is in labor. I can't go to her. She has a baby girl. I cannot see her. I cannot go to stay with her. Bert says he is so sorry.

It is the middle of the night and the pain is too much, eating at my husband.

Bert is having gruesome pain now. His dad takes him to the hospital. He calls in the morning. He is stable. I am drained. I am so tired.

I walk into the spare bedroom closet and bring down the family pictures we have treasured these past years. I sit in my nightgown looking at my handsome husband. My God, how the damn cancer has taken so much of him so soon. It feels good to look at the pictures. What a love he is.

Tony walks into the room and joins me in his pajamas. He wants to remember what his father looked like just a few short months ago. We cry. We know what is happening. Our hearts are mournfully frozen.

The phone rings. It is Bert's dad.

"Come quick. I don't think he has much time."

Tony and I throw on some clothes and jump in the car. As I drive, I assure Tony his dad will wait for us.

We arrive at the hospital and hurry to Bert's room. I cannot describe all that we saw. No wife or son should ever see the total ravages of cancer and death. He is gone. His eyes wide open. His piercing sky-blue eyes wide open! I try to close them. Bert's dad tells Tony to kiss him goodbye. Tony kisses his father on the forehead and runs from the room.

I ask Bert's dad if I can have some time alone with him. He says he will take Tony home.

I tell my sweet husband that I love him and that it is OK. "It's OK to go, Honey. Go toward the light. Jesus is waiting for you. You can go now. I love you so much. Go, Sweetheart."

There are no tears in me. Several people come into the room. It's all a blur. They put him in a frosted plastic bag. I glance over to the side of his bed and see a newspaper half open. There is an advertisement, and in big letters it reads: "THE BEST IS YET TO COME." I reach over, tear the words from the paper, and put it on his chest. I zip the bag shut. I walk with them to where they take him to keep him cold.

I don't know how I got home. I found myself sitting on our back porch sipping tomato soup. Bert's dad is not speaking. I don't know where Tony is.

I do not remember that when evening came I went to bed—alone. As I lay there, I heard him. He was standing next to the bed. I heard him breathing. It was Bert. I said, "My God Honey, you can't do this. You are scaring the hell out of me." He left.

The next day, a lot of calls are made, and people come. Then, there is the wake. When we arrive at the funeral home for the wake, Bert's parents are so upset. They do not want the coffin open. I agree to close it, but I need time. I need to say goodbye again, but I can't.

After the funeral service, the flurry of people and food, I am alone.

CHAPTER 8

JUST A FEW DAYS before Bert died, Yvette and my granddaughter, Hope, flew into Tucson. We sneaked the baby into Bert's hospital room. Bert was sitting in a large, overstuffed chair, and we kneeled down in front of him to show him this six-week-old baby girl. His face lit up like a Christmas tree, but he had the smile of a Cheshire cat. Yvette then rushed baby Hope out of the room. Bert leaned over and whispered in my ear, "That beautiful baby girl is part Indian." As usual, he was right.

Yvette and Hope will be going back to San Diego soon. I hold my precious, beautiful grandchild. She is incredible. She has fine, black, shiny hair, beautiful skin, and tiny, little, perfect features. She is healthy, and the most exquisite treasure there could ever be. Oh, thank you, God, for such a blessing.

The angels are singing in God's pink clouds.

I live alone now. Tony's mother has taken charge of where he lives. The house is too big for just me. I will stay for a while.

My days are orderly. I must keep things going. I don't know what will happen if I stop. I am going through papers and more papers, cleaning things out. I found a box in the bottom corner of Bert's closet. I rummaged through some papers and found two hundred dollars in cash. I laughed to myself because I found this very encouraging. But I am afraid to stop. I might feel the pain. I am trying to make sense of things—all kinds of things.

And then I drop to my knees and fall on my face. I will cry a river for the next six months. I will sit and look out the window and try to remember everything involving Bert in my life. I will go over it again and again. I think I am sorting things out, trying to understand what has happened. I do not eat much, and when I do, I stand over the kitchen sink and munch a few bites. I don't even bother to use a dish.

I have packaged up the rocks of Peli that Bert collected in Hawaii and sent them to a store where we had bought some things. I did not put a return address on the mailing label.

What will I do? I need help. I have found a group of people from hospice that meet. I have joined the group, but I cannot even speak. I join a group of people for widows and widowers, and again I am silent. I join a support group at the local church, but I am mute. There will be a lot of listening and crying for a while. When I do finally speak, I can't believe the story I tell of my grief is even mine.

Every spring, Bert and I went to the Fourth Avenue Street Fair. I saw the advertisement; it will be this week. I will go alone. I will walk around all the craft booths and enjoy myself. It will be good for me. I will be out in the sunshine and fresh air. I will treat myself to some melt-in- your-mouth Indian fry bread dripping in warm honey. I will go and I will enjoy myself.

Last year, when Bert's brothers and my future sisters-in-law came to town for a visit, we took them to the street fair. He always had such a good time with his brothers. They were very close. He was the big brother, and they looked up to him. His brothers admired his free will and envied the hippie lifestyle he once lived. He had even gone to the infamous Woodstock concert when he was sixteen.

As we all walked along the sidewalk to look at all the crafts, I wandered ahead. I realized we were separated, but I knew Bert and his brothers would catch up to me at some point. I found a spot to sit on the curb of the street to wait for them. I lit up a cigarette and looked up at the booth in front of me. An artist had his oil paintings on display. I began scanning each picture, then suddenly froze and gasped at the sight of one particular painting. What I saw was astounding. I could not believe my eyes. I crushed out my cigarette on the curb and walked toward that painting, my mouth wide open. The painting portrayed the artist's version of Jesus. It showed him from the chest up with a crown of thorns around his head. It was a close-up, larger-than-life image of a face I knew. It was Bert's face. When I could finally speak, I asked the artist how he had chosen this face for his painting. He said he used his brother-in-law as a model. I told him that this face is the face of my husband. He seemed curious and laughed. After a short conversation, I told him I must have this painting. The price was two hundred dollars. He would take my charge card. He wrapped the painting, and I sprang for the car. I wanted to put it in the trunk and surprise Bert and his brothers later.

When we got home that afternoon, I asked Bert and everyone else to go into the living room and sit down. I had covered the painting with a towel and leaned it up against a chair. Once everyone was seated, I made an announcement that I would like to show them what I had bought at the street fair—my find of the century. I asked them to please look at the painting, then, in a minute or so, tell me what they thought. Everyone laughed and waited for me to remove the towel.

I pulled the towel from the painting and circled the room. My eyes looked for each person's reaction. It was unanimous. They all said, "My God, it's Bert." Some months after Bert died, I sorely packed up the painting and shipped it to Bert's mother who was grieving terribly. She was so grateful. The conditions are that at Bert's parents' passing, the painting will come back to Bert's son, Tony.

It has been a year since we all went to the street fair, and now I will go alone.

This year, the street fair is not anything I expected it to be. The streets are bumper-to-bumper bodies. People pushing and shoving. There is no room to breathe. One woman with a stroller hollered at me, telling me I was rude, when I lost my balance in the crowd and bumped into her. Now stinging tears are welling in my eyes. I feel I am suffocating. People are angry. I need to get out of here, quick.

As I try to make my way to my car, I find long lines of people. I don't know how I got in front of this radio station's booth. Spin the wheel and if it lands on your birthday, you win one hundred dollars. People are telling me to spin the wheel. "It's your turn." I have no idea how I arrived in a position to spin the wheel.

Someone yells, "Let's go!" So I spin the wheel. The wheel stops and it is not my birthday, so I push my way through the crowd to find my car. As I walk, the date I had spun on the wheel keeps going over and over in my head. What is that date? It is so familiar to me. I will just find my car, go home, and figure it out.

When I got home, I needed to relax. I stretched out on the couch, and the date filled my thoughts again. I went to the kitchen to look at the calendar to see if I could make any sense of it. The date was circled on the calendar.

A few months back, Bert and I watched a faith healer by the name of Benny Hinn on television. We called in for personal prayer, and a woman prayed with us over the phone. We had hoped so much for healing. We wrote down the date that Benny Hinn was going to be in Phoenix. Bert and I decided we would go, but he died before we could.

I truly was in a state of shock. What did it mean? How is it possible that I spun that wheel and the date we hoped would be a trip to Phoenix for healing for Bert would come up on that wheel?

I knew then it was a message from Bert. He was telling me, "I am healed. I love you." An explosion of grief and love overwhelmed me, yet I felt a sense of peace.

Mother calls. She has had some rectal bleeding and is going to need a colonoscopy. I will take her to the doctor for this exam. Once more, I find myself in a conference room with a doctor. They show me the pictures of her colon. She has a huge tumor. I don't know how she can even function. The doctor wants to perform surgery as soon as possible. He is sure it is cancer. She will have a section of her intestine removed. She will have a colostomy for the rest of her life.

I don't know how I got through those next few weeks with Mom convalescing from her surgery. Some people from her church were there to help on occasion, and her sister came in from Ohio. Mom's sister, Mary, and her husband, Bob, arrived in a huge motor home and parked it in front of her home.

I can't remember helping my mother that much. I remember making my wonderful split pea soup and bringing her some. I could hardly see her every day. She went through chemo and radiation like a champ and didn't even lose her hair. She slept a lot and did not want to be disturbed. I can't help feeling that I should have been there for her more, but I just did not know how.

It is Thanksgiving time. Yvette will bring the baby and come home. Kirk will be here too. I will invite Mom, and anyone else I can think of, to make it a well-rounded day.

Yvette calls. "Mom, I am so sick. I don't know what is wrong. I have been to several doctors. They have not been able to help me. Mom, I can hardly walk, let alone take care of Hope."

I spring into action, call everyone that is coming for Thanksgiving dinner, and cancel it. I pack my bags, throw the turkey in the trunk, and head out to San Diego to help my daughter.

The trip is taking longer than my body can hold out. I must stop at a motel for the night. In the morning I grab a light breakfast and hit the road. I arrive at Yvette's apartment to find she has been taken to the hospital. Hope is at one of Yvette's friend's where she will be cared for.

"Someone tell me how to get to the hospital!" One of Yvette's friends gives me directions. I find the hospital and her room. I enter. My daughter looks like life has been drained from her whole being. She tells me she has been diagnosed with juvenile diabetes. She had gestational diabetes when she carried Hope. Now she has full-blown juvenile diabetes. I don't know what to think. I don't know what to do.

Yvette will be well enough to go home tomorrow with her new medication. She will need to take insulin shots four times a day. I will go back to her apartment and have her friend bring baby Hope over to me.

I don't know how we pulled it off, but we had a great Thanksgiving Day. Yvette was not concerned with the diabetes. She had learned to deal with it during her pregnancy. It was pure heaven taking care of my baby granddaughter. They will be fine. My daughter is such a strong woman.

When I returned home, my mother kept encouraging me to get out a bit. She urged me to try going to some of the singles functions she knew about and thought I should start with Parents Without Partners. I agreed to try it once.

It is Saturday, and tonight is the Parents Without Partners dance. I must go. I feel like I am dying—here alone every day and night. I have two wonderful kids and a granddaughter to live for. I force myself into the shower and adjust the water. I pull the plunger on the faucet and the water flows over me. A flood of hot tears streams down my face onto my chest. I can feel the tears meld with the shower water. Hurting. My soul is scourged with the emotional pain. My body wrenches in muscle spasms along my right side. I feel I must go to this damn function. I think I will die if I don't get out of this house. I don't care much what I wear or even if I look that great. I will just go.

I arrive at the building of Parents Without Partners, but I cannot get out of the car. I see a man smoking a cigar on the porch of the building. He must think I am nuts. I open the door, then shut the door until I finally fling my foot out of the car door and hit the sidewalk. I walk toward the building, and the man smoking the cigar gestures a hello to me.

I went in, paid my four dollars, and made a beeline to the ladies restroom. After checking my face and hair, I felt the courage to walk out. I could hear music playing in the background, one of my old fifties records. It sparked a feeling of better days. Days when I danced and had a good time. Days when I had no cares or worries. Happy days. My youth.

I walked into the main dance area and found a seat close to the door. Thank God. The sign said "Smoking Section." I lit up a cigarette and watched and listened. It wasn't long before a man approached me to dance. I will say yes. God knows I need the exercise. I danced and danced until my shoes kept falling off my feet. I hadn't worn what was suitable for what turned out to be a very vigorous activity.

Several of the men took me to the kitchen and lifted me onto the counter. One of them pulled out a kitchen drawer and found some string. They tied my shoes to my feet and grabbed me for the next dance. I did have a good time. I left a little early but decided dancing my woes away was not a bad idea.

I attended many singles' functions in the next few years, but eventually it got old. I was not out to replace Bert, and I just couldn't gel with any of the men I met. I did make a few friends though.

It seems I have simmered down a bit now. I mostly work, go home, get ready for work, and work some more. One day, in a horrible fit of pain, I asked God to either help me to find another man who I could live with the rest of my life or teach me to be happy all alone.

God has taught me to be totally happy alone.

I am getting older now, and for the first time, I am really angry at Bert. "I am turning gray; I am a little out of shape; and you are not here to experience the same thing." I do love him still, and I will sometimes be caught up in a moment when my heart pours torrential tears for him. I live now for my children and my grandchild.

CHAPTER 9

I SOLD THE HOUSE and bought something smaller, a townhouse in the same area of town. I need to deal with all things that go with a home now, on a smaller basis.

In the next few years there will be trips to San Diego to watch my growing granddaughter and visit my Yvette. They have their own apartment, as things never did work out with Hope's father. Kirk goes with me most of the time. We have wonderful days at Pacific Beach. The four of us are together and enjoy every minute.

Yvette is working on getting her credentials for teaching in California. Kirk is working for a man in Tucson who owns tons of real estate. He can remodel, paint, carpet, plumb, and do just about anything. Kirk works hard, and I know he plays hard.

The first summer I moved into my little townhouse, the monsoons hit me unmercifully. It was late afternoon on a Saturday in June of 2000. I was on the phone with a friend when it began to hail. I watched from my kitchen window as the water began to rise. I don't know what made me walk from room to room looking for any kind of damage from this storm, but I did. I noticed water coming in under the baseboard in one of the bedrooms. I ran from room to room on the north side of the house. Water gushed into every room. I frantically tried to move furniture out of that side of the house. The water just kept coming. The whole north side of my house was sitting in water. About this time, my sweet son showed up to trench the north side of the house. Water that comes in from the outside is black water—not healthy.

The storm was over, and the damage was huge. I called some-one right away because black water has pesticides, animal manure, dirt, bacteria, and God knows what else. If the house was not dried out quickly, I would be faced with a mold problem.

The local company I called specialized in water and fire dam-age. They came immediately. After they were finished with their es-timate and got my credit card, they worked through the night. The walls had to be gutted because the insulation was wet. They tore up the carpet and stacked all my furniture in the living room. Next, they sprayed a chemical to prevent mold, which made me nauseous, and brought in huge fans that would run for the next few days. It was over one hundred degrees outside, and we had to leave all the doors and windows open. A neighbor offered lodging to me for the night. Kirk said that none of this bothered him and he would sleep in the house.

I came home the next morning. As I walked through the house to assess the damage, I was overwhelmed. It was going to be very ex-pensive to put this all back to normal. I went out to my patio and sat down. My heart pounded, and I could not catch my breath. I became sick to my stomach. My legs felt like Jell-O, and my hands tingled. My mind raced. What is happening to me? I thought I was having a heart attack.

Kirk took me to the hospital. After hours in the emergency room, and many tests, I was told that I had had an anxiety attack. You could not prove that by me. Something was wrong with my body, not my brain.

I became more ill as the days went by. I could not eat or sleep. I ended up at Southern Arizona Mental Health. I was seeing a shrink!

He explained that I was having panic attacks and was depressed. He prescribed an antidepressant and medication for anxiety.

The next few weeks were pure hell. I prayed to either get well or die. I don't know what I would have done without Kirk. I woke up in the morning, stepped out of bed, and felt so ill that I fell back into bed and slept until noon. I tried to eat. I could only nibble.

The antidepressant was not working for me. I would need to try a different kind. Round in circles I went, pacing everywhere and scared to death. I was skin and bones. When would I feel better? It was weeks before I could sleep, eat, and not pace relentlessly.

Depression to me is when people have the blues. This was as close to feeling that I was in hell as ever could be. It took months before I was capable of getting through a day without feeling the imminence of death. My brain had gone haywire! Anxiety and depression had become predators on my mind. With counseling and the right medication, it took me almost a year to function normally.

I will manage this malady throughout my life. I live with depression and anxiety to this day but recognize its forces on me.

When I finally got my wits about me, I investigated the flooding of my home and found the causes—none of them mine. The neighbors had blocked the drainage swale with plants and rocks, and the builder had not built the foundation of the home to the proper height.

After years of paying a lawyer and fighting tooth and claw with insurance companies, neighbors, builders, the homeowner association, and God knows who else, I gave up. I lost big time. I had the house repaired, sold it, and bought another townhouse that was twenty years old. I knew that whatever could go wrong with this one already had.

The next few years were uneventful. Kirk and I did many things together. He came over sometimes, and we would rent a movie and pop popcorn. I loved having him around. He would fix whatever needed fixing, and I would cook him a great meal. He was so appreciative. He always said, "No one can compare to your cooking, Mom. You are the best cook in the world."

When I visited his home, it was never for long. He lived like a bum. He did not need anything and had nothing. His friends were usually buzzed on something, or what I call "sloppy drunk." These people were always hanging around his house. It was none of my business, and Kirk was always loving and good to me. I tried to get him to just think about rehab, but it was always, "No way." Finally, I settled for the fact that this is his life and I can't change it. *So butt out, Mom.*

In the back of my mind was an uneasy realization that someday he could die from his addictions. I was powerless.

CHAPTER 10

MY PLAN IS TO work until I can retire. There will be only short trips in the summer to visit my daughter and granddaughter in San Diego. They will visit me on holidays.

I begin to see a pattern when Yvette visits me. It troubles me, but I will not make judgments. She is a single, working mother and life is really tough for her now. I was a single mother for only two years. It was very complex, and one of the hardest parts of my life. When she comes home, she goes out with her old friends and sometimes stays out all night.

Hope, who is almost five now, is a pure pleasure to be with day in and day out. We always find something fun to do. We spend many hours playing our duets of "Heart and Soul" and "Chopsticks" on my piano. We study rocks and sea shells I have found, and we read together. She loves to play Slap Jack and spends hours in the tub or the community pool. She is a regular water baby!

Hope tells me I am her favorite person. She is so precious, beautiful, and wise beyond her years. The time we spend together is golden. It is even better than being a mother. I feel I have so much knowledge to share with her now. Things I was unable to share with my children when they were little. My time with my granddaughter is the most rewarding part of my life. She is the greatest gift God has given me.

As the years went by, and I visited Yvette and Hope in San Diego, I became more and more concerned. Yvette is experiencing panic attacks and high anxiety. Her drinking is progressing—not a good thing when you are diabetic. I can see that Yvette has a raging problem when she drinks now. I fear for her and Hope. My little girl has a huge problem. Oh, God, what do I do?

I hardly see Kirk at all now. Where is he?

He is in love, and he doesn't come by anymore. I miss him, but know how people react when they have been bitten by the love bug. I let go a little of my heart strings. *God, let him be happy.*

Christmas of 2003. Yvette and Hope come to visit. It is a short visit, and when they leave, I cry all day. I don't know why. I have an underlying feeling that I may never see them again.

Easter of 2004. I receive a call from Yvette's boyfriend. She is in the hospital. He says she took too much insulin. He feels it might have been a suicide attempt. My mind and body go into the fight or flight mode. I am sick. I feel panic rising inside me. *How in the hell can this be?* Yvette calls me from the hospital and says she is all right. She just became overwhelmed with teaching and everything else. She is coming home to Tucson as soon as possible. Hope will stay with her father who was married this past year.

Yvette never arrives. I wait. I call all her friends. I wait. I check with the police and hospitals. I wait. Finally, I receive a call from one of her old school girlfriends who tells me she is in the emergency room at our local hospital. I fly down to the hospital to find her being attended to by a doctor. He tells her she will be in intensive care. Her sugars are high and unstable. Her face is red, as if she had been sunburned. She tells me she went straight to Kirk's house when she arrived in Tucson. They had been drinking.

What kind of nightmare are we living? How did we get here? What is going to happen? What shall I do? God help us.

After five days in the hospital, Yvette comes home. The very moment we walk through the door of my house, the phone rings. It is a woman who wants to talk to Yvette. I tell her Yvette is too sick to talk to her and ask if we can call her back. She says to tell Yvette that a date has been set with a mediator in San Diego on Monday about custody of Hope. Hope's father has taken legal custody of her.

I relay the information to Yvette, who is on the couch still recovering from her hospital stay. She is yelling now, "He will pay! He will pay for this!"

He was never there to help her with Hope in any way through all these years. Now that he is married, he is trying to take custody! We will try to make it to San Diego by Monday.

We packed up all that we needed for the trip and arrived in San Diego the next evening. The mediation was scheduled for the next morning. We left Yvette's apartment with plenty of time to find the courthouse and the conference room. Hope's father was already in the room. His new wife sat across from us. Yvette was called in.

I went outside to smoke. When I returned, I heard Hope's stepmother talking with some people in the room, gloating about how she knew they would be granted custody of my grandchild. I did not say a word. She shut up the minute she realized who I was. In my heart I knew it would never matter how much this woman wanted to be the mother of my grandchild, she would never be her mother. Yvette is Hope's mother, forever. She can never change that.

An hour later, Yvette came out of the room and we drove home. She told me Hope's father will never get custody. She had been through many kinds of things with him before, and he always lost. There will be a court date soon, and she will be able to clear everything up at that time. I was devastated and emotionally drained from the past weeks and drove back to Tucson.

Yvette called me at home a week later and told me she had missed the court date. I cried, "How can that be?"

"Mom, it was on the mediator's papers we were given."

"I read all those papers before I left to come home, and I did not see a court date.'

"Mom, we both missed it. We were both in too much shock from the whole situation."

Dear God, what happens now?

Yvette lost custody of Hope. She can only visit her once a week at a place in downtown San Diego. The visits will be supervised, and Yvette must pay thirty-five dollars each visit. She says she will do this and will fight for her daughter. She is crushed.

Yvette talked to an attorney. It will be an uphill fight for years. She has become terribly discouraged, desperate, grievous, and physically ill. She is desolate without her little girl. She experiences panic and anxiety attacks. Yvette is paralyzed with fear and unable to even visit Hope at the specified times. She doesn't care if she lives or dies. I know firsthand how she feels. I have experienced this disease—depression and anxiety. It engulfs you when your mind suffers overwhelming loss, taking you to a dark, horrifying, and daunting place. She is broken and drinking daily. Yvette attempts suicide.

When the call came and I found where she had been taken, I called her to say I would help her, however humanly possible. Not to worry. Just get well. I will go out and stay with her a while.

It is Mother's Day. Yvette and I have a good day, but the underlying sadness of losing Hope hovers leaving us in deep despair.

I want to visit Hope before I go home and ask Yvette to arrange a time with Hope's father. He agrees that I can come and take Hope for a time. He calls back within hours and says I can only visit her at his home. I can only visit my granddaughter at her father's home? I know now that this custody thing has taken away my rights as a grandmother. How can they do that to us, to my precious granddaughter and me?

I arrive at Hope's father's home in the early afternoon. Her stepmother escorts me into the living room, and Hope comes to me. She looks different now. Not sparkly, not bubbly, not touching, not talking, not smiling, not anything. It's as if she is a Stepford child. I feel hollow. *Oh, God, what has happened to my beautiful grandchild?*

I ask if we might go out onto the patio, thinking we can be alone. Hope's stepmother seems totally in charge and leads the way.

Hope and I sat at the picnic table. She sat across from me and kept looking at the kitchen window. I could barely get her to speak. I was choked up, but knew I had a child's welfare to consider, and tried to engage her in some of the old fun things we used to do. Our hearts were just not in it. I asked her if I could just hold her for a while. She walked over to me, but I could feel her resistance. Oh, God, what have they done to her? Where is my sweet, wonderful Hope?

I choke back my tears and tell Hope I must go. I can hardly endure the changes I see in her. She is called into the house and returns with a letter. She asks me to give the letter to her mommy. I assure her I will. I hug her and drive back to Yvette's apartment.

Yvette met me at the door and asked how it went. I told her it was disturbing. The whole visit was strained. I gave her the letter from Hope. I could see how her heart was breaking. In turn, I read the letter. There was no way in hell my seven-year-old granddaughter could have written this letter. It said she felt abandoned and so forth. I am sure that letter was dictated to her to write, with the influence of her now guardians.

I recall, when Yvette had custody of Hope, how difficult it was sometimes to get Hope to go with her father on visits, how she cried that she did not want to go with him. Yvette and I would encourage Hope to go spend time with her daddy because he loved her. We wanted her to have that relationship.

My visits with Hope now are only in the presence of her father or stepmother. My phone calls, cards, and letters receive no response from her. It is as if someone is trying to erase Hope from my life.

I contacted several lawyers in San Diego about my grandparent rights. After much research, I found I have no rights. This whole damn scene is sick, sick, sick, and my hands are tied.

In the next few months, Yvette will slip into deep depression. She will hardly get out of bed. She does not work. She does not eat. She drinks. She will be hospitalized numerous times. I have pleaded with Hope's father and stepmother to allow Hope to visit her mother at the hospital. They refuse.

Yvette has totally given up on life. She calls me and cries about how sick she is, that she feels like she is dying. I become very ill myself. We are about as close to hell as you can get. It is a mentally dark and hopeless time, and it has affected our bodies as well.

One afternoon, I was on my knees praying. I cried so hard for God to help my daughter and granddaughter. I love them so. I am powerless. A strange feeling occurred, as though my being, my soul, was lifting from my body. Was God taking me home? I stood abruptly. I was still here. I was standing on my own two feet. I was not frightened.

I know God hears me and will guide me, He loves us so much. Many have suffered more. I surrender all to him. Only in his hands will anything happen. I am beyond being able to help anyone. I will stay positive. I will do the best I can every day.

Yvette calls me from San Diego. She is so very ill. Please, can I come out to her? I decide to wait.

It is Saturday morning. I am getting ready to go to an Al-Anon meeting. It is the only source of help I can find for these times. The doorbell rings, and I go to the window. It is Kirk. I let him in and hug him. It is so seldom I see him now that I hug him as much as I can. I still fear for him. His disease. Alcoholism is a disease.

He tells me he was so hungry last night he thought he would die. He still does not plan for groceries. I guess his booze comes first. I tell him I am getting ready to go to my meeting, and he can go to the kitchen and fix himself some eggs and toast. I will be out in a minute.

He asks if I can help him out with his mountain bike. It has a flat tire and needs a new inner tube. I tell him, "Of course I will, on the way to my meeting."

I ask him to come into my bedroom and listen to the message his sister left on my machine. She is crying again about how ill she is and how she feels she is dying.

At first, I thought his respond was a laugh, but then I saw big tears streaming down his face. I was hoping he had a solution. I am very ill from this disease that is ruling our lives, mentally and physically. But I tell him I'm not worried. Yvette is in Jesus's hands. There is nothing we can do. If she dies, the Lord will be there to take care of her. I ask him how he is doing, and he replies, "Mom, you never have to worry about me. God takes good care of me."

We left for the store.

When we finished shopping and got into the car, Kirk began to tell me how much in love he is. How I must meet Janet. He says he wants to get married and have children. We had just bought food for his new cat, and I said, "Kirk you can't even feed your cat. What makes you think you can have a baby?" I want him to think about his disease. He gives me a hug, and I hug him back.

I dropped him off near his home. He rode off on his bike, and I went to my meeting.

After the meeting, I decided to get some groceries for Kirk. He has such a good heart, and the damn alcoholism is his only real problem. I will not give him money, but I don't want him to starve. I bought a whole bunch of things I knew he could cook and would fill him up—a big bag of potatoes, a box of macaroni, a gallon of milk, hamburger, hot dogs, and all kinds of other things. I drove over to his house.

I walked up the makeshift stairs to his trailer and hollered in for him to help me unload my trunk. "I have groceries," I yelled.

He is sitting on his couch watching football. He looks stoned or something. I am pissed. I start unloading the trunk, myself. He joins me, and within a few minutes, we are done. He wants me to look at his cat. I tell him I have to go. He begs me to stay a while, but I am angry. It is the middle of the afternoon and he is stoned.

He walks me to my car, and I get in. I look at him standing there, looking down at his feet, like a little boy who has been bad or is ashamed. He walks to my car and kisses me gently on my left cheek. I say goodbye and drive home.

I came home from work on Monday. As I undressed, I played my answering machine message. It was Kirk. I was in my walk-in closet hanging up my clothes as I heard him speak. He said "Mom . . ." After that everything was slurred, as if he had been drinking a lot. I said to myself that this did not sound like Kirk. Whenever he called me, he was upbeat and always left a short, sweet message. I made a mental note to listen to the message again later. I thought, *Oh hell, he is drunk. I will deal with this later. I will try to go down to his place sometime after dinner to see what's up.* I was so tired of the damn effects alcohol was having on my family. I did not go see him that night. I was tired. I just went to bed.

In the next few days, I decided that I should get out to San Diego to help Yvette. She would at least eat while I was there, and that is a good start. It was Thursday, and I had been at Kirk's on Saturday. I wanted to drop off some medicine for his stomach. When we had last been together, he told me he had been fighting heartburn for weeks. And I wanted to leave him a note that I was going to San Diego to help Yvette.

I arrived at his trailer, and he was not home. I went inside. There was something different. I could not put my finger on it, but it felt kind of sad or like something was missing. It was just strange. Everything was neat and tidy. But I could only think about getting on I-10 and driving to San Diego, so I left the medicine and the note on his card table.

I had been at Yvette's for only a couple of days when the phone calls started. They were from friends of Kirk's wondering where he was. I called my neighbor in Tucson who had a key to my house. I asked him to go over and see if Kirk was there. There had been many times in the past when I left town that he went to my house to eat and veg out.

The neighbor called me back and said there was no trace of anyone having been at my house. I begin to feel the old panic attack sneak in on me. I tell it I am here helping Yvette and can't be bothered with wherever the hell Kirk is.

I told Yvette to call her father in Tucson and have him check the jail, the hospitals, and the morgue. I truly felt these were the places where an alcoholic might end up. I learned from rehab, with Kirk years ago, that most alcoholics/addicts end up either in prison, go insane, or they die.

I went for a morning walk. I had recently been diagnosed borderline diabetic, and part of my care was to watch my diet and exercise regularly. So, I walked thirty minutes a day. I felt it was saving me mentally as well as physically.

As I returned from my walk and approached Yvette's apartment, I saw her standing outside in her nightgown. When I reached her she said, "Mom, I have bad news . . . Kirk is dead."

I don't remember what I said to her, but it was something to the effect of, "How do you know this?" She replied that Jake, the landscaper Kirk worked for, asked his girlfriend to call around to find Kirk. She called the morgue, and they had a positive ID on him.

I walked into Yvette's apartment and told her I was going to get gas for my car, then I was going home. She said she was coming too. I told her she was too sick. She said, "He is my brother, and I am going with you."

There are no tears; there is nothingness. A big, fat void.

I yelled at Yvette, "You are the only thing I have left. Please, for God's sake, get it together." She started packing. I grabbed my purse and headed to the corner gas station to fill up the car. My damn card would not work at the pump. I had to go inside and give the attendant my card to hold while I filled the tank. I went back inside and stood at the counter waiting for him to process my gas charge. It seemed as if the world had stopped. I wasn't even there. It was as if I never existed. If he only knew the news I had just received, would he believe it? He handed me my card, and I left. I returned to the apartment. Yvette was nearly ready to go.

We packed the car and headed to the freeway. I asked Jesus out loud, "Please drive my car for me. Take us back to Tucson, now."

CHAPTER 11

WE DROVE BACK TO Tucson stopping only once. Yvette was on her cell phone the whole time gathering information. She talked to her father, who confirmed that Kirk was at the Forensic Science Center. He would meet us at my house in the evening. She also talked to her friends, and Kirk's friends, and anyone else who might have any information back in Tucson. We arrived at my house. The kid's father, Bill, came over about an hour later.

We have to make the funeral arrangements tomorrow, Friday. Where was Kirk's body to be taken? We decided he should be taken to Evergreen Mortuary. The service will be held there, and if he is cremated, his ashes can be placed on Bert's grave. I knew I was going to be there someday when I bought the plot for Bert, and that made me happy. Now I would put my son there before I die?

Bill said he would make the calls and let us know what time to be at the funeral home tomorrow. He explained that Kirk was found on the railroad tracks at Ruthrauff Road and Casa Grande Highway on Monday night, September 27.

"That was the day he left a drunken message on my phone," I said.

Bill said he had left a message on his phone too.

I had seen Kirk walking with a white, plastic grocery bag in each hand as I drove to work the day he left the message on my phone. I honked my horn, and he raised his bags in his hands to acknowledge me. That was the day he died!

Bill said the police told him that Kirk's mountain bike was lying on the tracks, and his body must have been in front of the bike. The train conductor did not see anyone around and did not stop. Kirk was run over by a train. That night, before I went to bed, I fell to my knees and belted out sobs that came from deep within my soul.

From here on, I don't remember much. It seems I was not even in my body. We met with the funeral director the following day. The arrangements were made, and we picked out an urn to hold Kirk's ashes for interment. After the details were finalized, we were told his body had arrived.

The funeral director said he had Kirk's personal effects and placed a clear ziplock bag on the table. I opened it. Inside were a gold chain necklace and a penny. Yvette asked if she could keep the necklace. I nodded yes and picked up the penny.

"No one can say my son did not have a cent to his name," I said.

I turned to the funeral director and insisted on seeing my son now. He told me I could not see him. By law I was not allowed to go back to the room where Kirk was.

I pleaded, "Let me see my son."

The director seemed very concerned and asked me to please wait until they had him ready. I finally agreed.

Saturday, we bought some nice clothes for Kirk's viewing. Yvette brought a Dale Earnhardt racing hat he had loved for him to wear and one of Hope's stuffed animals for him to hold. I took the clothes and a picture to the funeral home and asked them to call me as soon as he was able to be viewed.

Sunday, Kirk's obituary was in the paper. October 10—Bert's birthday. *My God, are you trying to tell me something, Honey? Is my baby boy with you?*

Monday morning I was getting cleaned up when I heard Kirk's voice in my head, "Momma, you can come see me now. They did a pretty good job."

Later that morning the funeral staff called and said we could see Kirk that afternoon.

We all arrived at the funeral home together, Yvette and I, Bill and my mother. We were ushered into a large room. A casket was placed along the wall.

I went to him first. I looked at him. I touched his forehead. It is him. I had hoped there had been a mistake, maybe it would not be Kirk in this casket. *My God, it is my boy.* This is different than when Bert died. Totally different. I expected Bert to die. Kirk is thirty-five and lying in this coffin.

Involuntary gasps and sobs come from my mouth, "My son, my son, I love you. Oh Kirkie, I love you."

Others are beside me now, but I am not aware of what anyone else experiences. I see that my mother needs to sit down. We are quiet. I want to stay by Kirk's side forever. *Oh God.* Growls of grief come from deep inside me. I sit down.

Tony, Bert's son, my stepson, enters the room. We are so happy to see him. He had to take a cab and apologizes for being late. We lead him over to Kirk. I don't remember anything else.

The next morning, Tuesday, was Kirk's funeral. We had met with the pastor on Saturday. There would not be a eulogy for fear that one of Kirk's drinking buddies might choose to get up and speak, just a message from the pastor.

Yvette and I are the first to arrive. I go straight to Kirk. I don't know what to say. I recall some wonderful times we had. I tell him I love him. I stay with him as long as I can. I tour the room. It is full of flowers. I read the cards. The wonderful things they say about him. Kirk was the "go-to guy." If you needed your car fixed or you were moving—any request a friend had—Kirk would help. There are flowers and notes from people I have not heard from for years; it makes me cry.

Janet, the love of my son's life, approaches the coffin. She is the only girl he was ever excited about. He told me she had the most beautiful hair. He wanted me to meet her. He wanted to marry her. Now I am seeing her for the first time. She is petite and slender with a small, pale face. Her long, thick, light-brown hair is wind-blown and slightly curly. You could see her hair a mile away. She stomps her feet repeatedly and cries bitterly. I go to her to try to console her, but she seems more receptive to Yvette.

Kirk's old employer Ernie is here. He is a kind man, and Kirk had felt Ernie was like a father to him. My son worked for Ernie for years. He remodeled and repaired Ernie's properties to get them ready to rent. Someone told me that Ernie's son Josh died the day before Kirk. Kirk had told me about Josh's illness and said he felt sad. Josh was in his mid-twenties and dying of testicular cancer. I felt that, right there, would be enough for Kirk to tie one on.

A young man in casual dress approaches the coffin where I am standing. I notice him kind of flinch and step back. I ask him who he is. He says his name is Jake, and Kirk had worked for his landscape company. I get a very bad vibe. In my mind I hear Kirk saying, "I no like," which he used on occasion. We exchange a few words, and I ask him if he will call me. I want to find out if he might have any information relevant to Kirk's death. He says he will. Jake steps closer to the coffin and looks Kirk over. I feel it is a little odd. When I look again at Kirk, it is as if he is frowning. It was intense.

A half dozen of Kirk's drinking buddies are sitting together. They are in jeans and T-shirts. One is drunk. I do not talk to them much.

Kirk's buddy who was drunk at the funeral will die of liver damage and pancreatitis in the next year.

The service is starting. I must sit down.

I sit between Tony and Yvette. I remember when Tony was little, how he looked up to Kirk. He called him his big brother. Janet sits with my mother through the service. They hold each other. Later, I ask Janet if she will please call me. She says she will.

After the service, we had cold cuts at my house, and Yvette was very busy serving everyone. I did not do anything. I sat and talked to some of our old neighbors, the ones the kids had grown up with. It was as if Kirk was there the whole time.

I don't know when they all left. I am glad Yvette is here with me. Tomorrow, Wednesday, Kirk will be cremated. Thursday, we will meet for his interment at Bert's grave.

Only the immediate family is graveside. They bring Kirk's urn in a big hearse. We each have a turn to say something. I don't remember what anyone said.

I could only say, "I don't know what happened to you. I love you, I love you, I love you. I will not suffer because I know that is not what you would want." Then I sang, "Jesus loves you, this I know, for the Bible tells me so." We sang that song together when he was little.

CHAPTER 12

MY ONLY SENSE OF being now lies in questions, questions, questions. I have so many burning questions. I don't know where to start.

The next few days, Yvette and I stayed home trying to make some sense of it all. She made calls to people trying to find out what happened. Bill requested a police report and the autopsy report. We visited the specified area where they said Kirk died. I knew he didn't die in the place we were looking. I could just feel it. We went to Kirk's trailer and found nothing we could take home as a memento.

Later, on my own, I went back to his trailer and found the Lord's Prayer Kirk had written the best he knew how inside an empty stereo speaker. It reassures me. I know where he is.

I spent the next few days walking up and down the railroad tracks trying to make sense of what happened. Again, I felt out of body, an empty shell, nonexistent. At one point, a train came. I stood in horror as it passed. It was so huge; it was so powerful; it was so loud. *My God!* I trembled; I could not breathe. I looked at the wheels rolling over the track. What damage they might do! The ground shook and all of the loudness and powerfulness of the train shot through me. *God, God, God, how could you let this happen to my boy? I want my boy back, I want my boy back. Did he suffer? Oh God, oh God.*

After a few days, Janet called. Thank God, I have so many questions. She sobbed so much I could hardly understand her. I asked her the same questions over and over again.

My first question was, "Had they had a fight? Were they breaking up?"

"No," she replied. "There was no reason for Kirk to be at the railroad tracks. None!"

There is nothing at those tracks but on and off-ramps to Interstate 10. Through the conversation I found out that she lives only a few blocks from Kirk's trailer. They had been together all day Sunday, the day after I had brought groceries to Kirk. They had a beautiful day, and he walked her to the bus stop for work the next morning. Monday, the day he died.

Janet said, "Kirk had given up the drugs and was doing a fine job. I could not be around anyone who did drugs. He was trying hard to quit drinking. I told him I would move in with him sometime. He asked me if he came by tomorrow to help me move in, would I do it? I said yes. I loved him so. Kirk booted his friends out to change his life, and they were angry. I feel they might have hurt him."

Janet and I talked back and forth for about an hour.

Some of Kirk's old friends started calling, and I kept gathering information. One school chum said the pickup truck parked on the side of Kirk's trailer was Jake's, the landscaper. Jake owed Kirk money, and Kirk had kept the truck as collateral. I asked this friend if he thought Jake might have hurt Kirk. He said it is common knowledge that if you want someone hurt or killed, Jake is the man to see. Kirk could have been killed in the parking lot of a little neighborhood bar, called the Firelite, where they could buy pints of liquor.

At this point, I am going out of my mind. I can't believe all the information that may be relevant to my son's death. I am in agony, but I want to get to the bottom of all of this.

Another girlfriend of Kirk's called out of the blue one Saturday morning. I asked her what she thought about Kirk's death. She felt that Jake was an evil person and that anything was possible. She also told me that one night about a year ago, when she and Kirk had gotten really drunk, he had said that it all had to end someday. He had bad feelings about his future and said he would end it all if he had to, by lying on the railroad tracks.

The stories drive me to my knees. I am in a whirl of grief and depression. I am hurt beyond what I feel anyone can ever take. I am confused, and I want answers.

It has been weeks now, and Jake has never called, so one afternoon I called him.

"I am trying to piece together what was going on with Kirk before he died," I explained.

He answered abruptly, "The Monday Kirk died, he came over to my house in the morning as usual to see what work there was to do. I had a flat tire, so we couldn't work. We put on the spare and took the truck to a tire shop. We waited around a few hours at the shop, and Kirk had a beer from the Circle K next door. All Kirk talked about was Janet. Janet this, and Janet that. We got the tire fixed, went back to my house, and just bullshitted the afternoon away. Kirk left about eight p.m. and rode his bike home. That was the last time I saw him."

I would later find out that the train passed over Kirk at 9:37 p.m.

I asked Jake if he owed Kirk money, and he said he did, about one hundred dollars. I asked if he would give the money to me. He said he knew where I lived and would bring it by. He never showed up.

It has been a few weeks now, and the police report arrives. There is no preparation for any parent to read a police report about how their child died. As I read each page, the tears roll like a raging river from my eyes. I have to stop to purge the pain with tears and start reading again. I must have read the report three times. I need someone else to read it for me. It is incomprehensible. I cannot digest the information. I am so distressed. I need to know what happened.

I finally took the report to the counselor I saw when Yvette had attempted suicide. Maybe she could help me make sense of it. I burst with grief as she read it aloud for me. I cried and cried. I noted the counselor cried too as she read. She felt that Kirk had committed suicide, and he did not want me to know. He was looking out for his mom.

He had been run over by a train. The female engineer did not stop. She saw a bike lying across the tracks and thought it was a prank. She called a friend later to see if a pedestrian had been involved. Her friend found the body and called the police. The report was lengthy. There must have been twenty police officers at the scene. They found Kirk facedown in a crumpled ball. His right forearm and hand were found twenty feet down the track. His right leg and foot were hanging by a tendon. A hat, sweatshirt, and shoes were all found in different places. Part of his bike was found many feet down the track. The report said his death was consistent with body tumbling—usual in a train accident. In his back pocket was a crushed pint of Hiram Walker Peppermint Schnapps.

I must walk and walk and walk and walk. I cry and cry and cry. As I walk, each day I hear the damn train whistle again and again, haunting and tormenting me. *God, make that damn train whistle stop.* I had never heard the train whistle before. Now I hear it everywhere I go. I have no idea how I am going to work every day. I have no idea how I am doing the daily things one does. I sit each night in my chair in my room with a candle lit near a picture of my boy.

"Oh, God, I thought you would always take care of my children. I hate you. I hate you God. Do you hear me? I hate you!"

It is about six weeks now since Kirk died, and I receive the autopsy report. I go through the same process of grief as I read this new information. It seems almost every bone in his body was broken. Lacerations, contusions, abrasions, and blunt impact injuries to the head, torso, and extremities. His blood alcohol was very high.

I went to my computer to look up information about blood alcohol levels. I find that his level of intoxication was equivalent to being able to undergo surgery without anesthesia. I have a morbid sense of relief. Maybe he didn't even feel the pain. Most likely Kirk was in the blackout stage that alcoholics experience.

I have gone over the information about Kirk's death a thousand times now. Janet, Yvette, and almost everyone else do not buy suicide. Before his death, Kirk was happier than any of us had ever seen him. He was in love. He could not stand the sight of blood. Yvette knew him better than anyone else. She had seen him both drunk and stoned. He was not suicidal. He would become angry and belligerent at times, but he would not commit suicide.

Voter Registration called today about Kirk's application. He had always used my phone number for things like that. Kirk registered to vote, for God's sake!

Everything made me wonder about Jake. Yvette told me that when Jake called her in San Diego to inform her of her brother's death, he had said, "I have good news and bad news. We found Kirk, but he is dead."

I decide to call the pathologist to ask whether or not they could tell if Kirk was alive when the train crossed over him. The pathologist replied that I must watch too many forensic television shows. I think to myself, *You son of a bitch*. And I ask again, "Can't you tell about when he died?' The answer is no.

Next, I decided to call Jake. He was with Kirk the whole day he died. I rang him up and asked if he thought Kirk might have had enemies that would have put him on the railroad tracks? He said that Kirk did not have any enemies. I told him I had called the doctor, who did the autopsy, to find out if Kirk was alive when he was run over by the train. There was no response. Then I told him that I was just wondering; I was trying to make sense of it all. We said goodbye.

Within a few minutes, Jake called back.

He said, "You've really got me wondering. Was the doctor able to tell if Kirk was alive when he was hit by the train?"

I said, "No, he thought I must have seen too many forensic TV shows." We ended with a curt OK and goodbye. That was my last conversation with him.

I began searching for someone to help me find the answers I needed. Suicide? Possible murder? Accident?

I called the officer in charge of Kirk's case—the officer who was there that night; the officer who saw my son's body. Surely he can answer some of my questions. It will be days before I receive a call back. The officer I need to talk to only works evenings.

Finally, Detective Copfer called. He listened to me and answered most of the questions I had. My first question was whether he knew if Kirk had any kind of police record. He indicated he had already checked on this, and no, Kirk did not have a police record. I explained that we did not feel this was a suicide, and we would like him to question some people. He agreed to talk to Janet, Jake, and a few of Kirk's friends. It will be weeks before he calls back.

Detective Copfer finally called with the information he collected. The only person we discuss for a long while is Jake. Jake told the detective a totally different story than what he told me. Kirk's friend, who called me and said it was common knowledge that Jake was the guy to see if you wanted someone killed or hurt, was never available for Detective Copfer to question. He did talk to Kirk's old girlfriend who confirmed that Kirk had said he had a bad feeling about his life and would end it all by lying on the railroad tracks. The detective did not seem hopeful that he would be able to gather much more information.

A few months down the road, Detective Copfer called to tell me that Jake had been arrested for domestic violence, that Jake is not his real name, and that he has a record as long as one's arm. He hit his girlfriend so hard her eye popped out of its socket. She was filing charges. She told the police that Jake said he would kill her, just like he did Kirk. Later, she recanted this information. The police won't do any more. Their facts determine it was a suicide.

I am in so much pain. I am saturated in grief, depression, and anxiety. I must find help—an outlet for my misery. Guidance. I will seek help. I must find a way to get through this nightmare. Someone tells me about Compassionate Friends, a group that meets twice a month. Parents who have lost a child. I will start there.

CHAPTER 13

THE COMPASSIONATE FRIENDS MEET mid-town at a church. I arrive early. The meeting is held in a huge room. Inside the door is a table with cookies and coffee. The seats are arranged in a big circle. I sit down. A woman approaches me and asks if she can make a name tag for me. I respond with yes. I find a seat near the door. I don't know why, maybe to leave early if I feel the need. It isn't long until the room fills with people. Some are happy to see each other, chatting and hugging.

A man opens the meeting saying, "If everyone will have a seat, we can get started. Welcome. We are glad you found us, but we are so sorry for the circumstances that bring us together. We understand your pain; we hope our unconditional friendship and understanding will help you through your grief. There are many here with mixed emotions. Attending this meeting for the first time takes courage, but for many it is the first step toward healing. This may seem overwhelming, so we encourage you to come to several meetings to give yourself a chance to become comfortable."

Next, a wooden butterfly is passed around to each person. Each person states the child's name, how that person died, and the age at death. I listen intently. What had all these people's children died from? How many people lose a child?

I will learn later that about twenty-five percent of the population will lose a child.

There are people who lost a child to crib death, illness, an accident, killed in action in the war, suicide, and murder. Where did I fit?

Most of them tell a little bit about their child, and some are too emotional to speak. I cannot speak when the butterfly is passed to me. I can only gush tears and look down at the floor. I feel an arm go around me. I don't know who the lady is, but it is good. I know I am in the right place.

Eventually we broke into smaller groups where people could say what was on their minds. In each group there was someone who had been dealing with grief a lot longer than most of us and could talk about what is working for them.

After a series of meetings, I really did get the whole picture. I was able to say, "I am Kirk's mother. I don't know how he died. He was run over by a train. He was thirty-five." I think to myself, *Oh, God, why do I even have to be in this position?*

Because of these meetings, I learned that I am really not doing so badly. There are mothers who did not get out of bed for three years after their child died. There are people who are religious and had cursed God as I had. There are people who wished they were dead, as I did. All of the things you never think you will have to endure are discussed. We all came to these meetings from the same place. I am learning that I will work through the grief. There is no shortcut. Someday I will be able to put Kirk in a special part of my heart and still live.

In the spring, Compassionate Friends had a potluck and balloon release in a local park. Each parent wrote a message on a card attached to a helium balloon, then there was a mass release. I wrote on Kirk's card, "I LOVE YOU. I MISS YOU. I DON'T KNOW HOW I CAN LIVE WITHOUT YOU." When I released my balloon, I watched it go up into the sky until it became a small dot and I could no longer see it. I know he got my message. I know he loves me. I know he is not suffering. I know it does not matter how he died, and I know that someday I will be with him again.

I know God forgives me for being angry with him.

I also felt the need to visit Homicide Survivors. This group of people has lost loved ones to violence. Murder.

There I learned that you need to stay on the police to get them to process your case. Homicide Survivors is like an advocate. They work with the police. They make posters with your loved one's picture and offer rewards for information. They said you can get a lot of information this way.

Most of the people in Homicide Survivors are not only grief-stricken but angry. There are counselors at each meeting. It seems that the fight for justice is a long, hard process, and sometimes, if there is a trial, the perpetrator gets off with a light sentence. It is far more than most people can take. The process of justice most times becomes a dead end.

It was a dead end for me. When Homicide Survivors contacted the police officer in charge of Kirk's case, they learned that his death was recorded as a suicide. This made me angry. They would never know for sure unless they really investigated his case. Based on their information, they had not done that. I felt like Kirk's case was a lost cause. I could not get them to do any more than they had done. I pray I am not letting Kirk down.

In the next year or so, I go through terrible mind crazes. What if I would have gone down to his house the day he left the message on my phone machine when he sounded so drunk? I might have been able to save his life. This will kill me if I am not careful. I still have a daughter and granddaughter I dearly love. Kirk did not have a phone. He always called from a pay phone or somebody's cell phone. I know I would have called him back if I could have. But maybe not.

Oh, God, why didn't I go to him that night just to see what was going on? I have kicked myself over and over again because of that last conversation with him.

I said, "How can you think about getting married and having a baby when you can't even feed your cat." Even with my pissed-off attitude that day, he was forgiving and loving. He kissed me on my cheek before I pulled out of his driveway.

If he committed suicide, why did I not see it coming? Was I dumb? Did all the years and things I learned in Al-Anon stop me from helping him? If he was murdered, the person who committed this crime should not be on the streets! How could I help him?

"I love you, Kirk. Forgive me."

I hear his voice in my mind saying, *Mom, it was an accident.*

Or am I just going mad? I doubt my sanity. For months I read other people's stories about losing their child. I gather many thoughts. I resolve that I will always think of him every day. That I will always love him. That I am still living and that there is an afterlife.

After Bert died, I heard his voice talking to me on many occasions in the following years. It was him; it was his voice in my mind. What he said was always something only he would say. This is why I knew it was him and not my imagination. I asked him once why he wasn't in heaven. He said he was in heaven, but he is still in my heart. The same thing has happened since Kirk died. I know that all people have the capacity to hear from loved ones who have died. They are just too afraid to use it. Both Bert and Kirk told me that where they are now is unbelievable, and I would not be able to comprehend it—that it is wonderful beyond anyone's wildest dreams. I believe them. But they are there and I am here. It seems like it will be forever until I am with them again.

I ask Kirk to come and sit with me sometimes in the evenings. I really feel he is there. I feel both he and Bert come around from time to time. They are only a dimension away. It is always relieving to feel their spirits near me. I enjoy the things they tell me and point out to me. But I miss their bodies.

Kirk has told me on many occasions that his death was an accident. I figured he would say that to make me feel better, and that he did not die of suicide or murder. I know it doesn't matter how he died, the result is still the same. I did feel I had a right to know how he died, but that is changing now. I will always love him no matter how he died.

As time has passed, I have come to understand that when it is our time, it is our time. I feel we all come from the same place, the heart of God, and we will all go back to the same place. Death is only stepping into another dimension. There is no pain. There is only love. We will know each other again. Everything that happens in our life is as it should be. We have choices in how we react to all of life's trials. Some are harder than others, but we can find a place called peace.

My outlook on working, money, health, people, relationships, and just general living has all changed. Losing a child will always be one of the worst traumas a human being will experience. Somehow we find a way to exist, then live again. We never forget the ones we lose. We fight for the ones that are still here. We just do the best we can. We must be gentle on ourselves. We must give ourselves the time we need for our hurts. We do the best we can each day, then for no reason at all, the pain returns. It's OK. It is really OK. It is a process.

I don't think we are here to learn lessons. We are here for only one reason—to live life no matter how long that may be. We are loved. We are never alone. There are many twists and turns in the road of life. I hate the saying that God never gives you more than you can handle. God doesn't have a damn thing to do with it. I hate the saying that when one door closes, another door opens. We decide which doors to open and close.

Losing a child to death truly becomes a test of one's faith, but not a test from God.

The pink clouds of comfort we all pray for and feel we are promised from God come from our acceptance. Willingness to accept is the hurdle we face. When acceptance happens, pain recedes like a crashing wave from the ocean washing back into the sea, again, again, and again.

I believe that deep inside of each one of us is our soul, and that we choose how we use it. We can never make wrong decisions, just mistakes. It's just part of the deal, living.

I have loved ones still here in my life. I am happy to be around to know I will have some wonderful experiences in the future, and I will always have fond memories. I thank God for his great gift of love. I pray he guides each of us. I know that most of life is good.

· C H A P T E R   1 4 ·

You will be not cured, but . . . one day—an idea that will
horrify you now—this intolerable misfortune will become
a blessed memory of a being who will never again leave
you.

-Marcel Proust Letters

I KNOW I AM powerless over alcohol. My counselor told me that
my codependency is life threatening for me. I have turned my life
over to God. I have put all my troubles in the hands of the Lord, but
the nightmare does not end.

Yvette seems to be hanging on to life by a thread. She is still so
ill. She tries and fails. I have started going to Alcoholics Anonymous
to try to understand what goes on in the mind of the alcoholic. I have
read the "Big Book" of Alcoholics Anonymous. All that they say about
this disease is true. It is cunning and baffling.

I worry about Hope. What must she be going through not having her mother now?

Kirk died in 2004. In March of 2005, I walked off my job. I am
unable to deal with any more stress. I have become easily irritated. I
have tried to go back to work several times and have walked off those
jobs too.

I will allow myself to take the time I need for now. I will use
what little money I have left from Bert's life insurance to live on. I
was hit hard in the stock market in 2003. I only have a small amount
of my investments left for my retirement. I really don't give a damn.

I need this time. I will sell my house if I have to. I need to get a hold on life, on living.

Each day I will do something positive. Each day I will entrust all to God for him to control. Each day I will walk and eat right. Each day I will do the best I can. But fear underlies my whole being.

CHAPTER 15

God, grant me the serenity to accept the things I cannot change, courage to change the things I can, and the wisdom to know the difference.

-The Serenity Prayer

THERE DOES NOT SEEM to be any way to help your alcoholic. You are damned if you do, and you are damned if you don't.

You love your alcoholic. Your alcoholic makes you angry. Why can't they whip this problem and have a life like anyone else? People do make it! Many don't. Why?

Alcoholism is a disease. Then why isn't there a cure? Alcoholism is hereditary. Can't we just lock them up somewhere until they lose the desire to drink? What has to happen to get them to change their life?

How does one try to live one's life with the daily insanity and horrors that go with loving an alcoholic? Do you shut them out of your life? How do you do that when you love them?

I have learned that alcoholics feel they are a low form of life each day. Every day they face failure. We must then let them know that no matter what, they are loved. It is a disease. God almighty, are we in the dark ages or something that we can't help these poor souls? They have been around since liquor was first invented. They are everywhere! Just take a look!

The reality is that my daughter may not make it. She may die too.

Someone must be around to tell her daughter that her mother did love her, but she was sick.

I will walk. I feel the warm penetrating sun on my back, yet I shiver. I see the clear, blue sky. The light streams through the tall trees. I am not a fortune teller. I do not know what the future holds. I know that God is here. It is still a beautiful world.

CHAPTER 16

If you can give something a name and shape, you can have power over it. If it remains nameless and shapeless, it will continue to have power over you.

-Native American Proverb

MY EMOTIONS ARE OVERPOWERING. I don't know what it is that makes me feel so bad, really bad. I need to do something or I will go mad. I need to identify what it is that is so desolate, so black, so morose, pulsating through my body. I always feel the pain in my body, but I know its source. My brain.

I'm running on empty. I must dig at the source of the festering pain and anguish going on in my being. I cannot kill myself. But the suffering must take a turn toward understanding in order to extinguish the fire of the pain.

What is it? What the hell is eating at my will to strive to survive and live?

Kirk was a loving son, but his disease was an evil to be reckoned with. Cunning and baffling. I am starting to remember the times he was drunk or high. I could not handle it. I was glad when he just went to sleep. It was at these times that his behavior would become unbelievable. The chemicals had control of his mind. He would become boisterous, belligerent, obnoxious, poisoned. On many occasions I told him he could not stay with me. I did not care where he went, but I couldn't live like this.

I don't know where he resided at these times, but I know his so-called buddies never took him in. I was on my knees praying for him.

I love him, but he needed to take care of himself. Letting him flop at my house only contributed to his disease. So, unlike some of his alcoholic friends' parents, I booted him out. His alcoholic best friends are still alive. Kirk is not.

Yvette is going down the same path Kirk took, but she is not belligerent. I take her in for short intervals but always know it is best for her to be on her own too.

The pain is caustic, toxic, and lethal. It is guilt. *Oh, God, it is guilt.* Did I contribute to my son's death and my daughter's disease?

A torrent of sorrow fills me now. I must release it. I know why I feel so bad, but I am unable to find any consolation. I think of killing myself. *Oh God, Oh God.* Should I have helped them more? Oh God, I could not take their pain. No matter what I did, there was never any improvement. I am defending myself now. There is no mercy, no end, no way to purge my grief. I have dealt with these damn addictions in my children for years. I went to counseling; I went to Al-Anon meetings for years. I read about the disease and how it affects the whole family. Why the damn guilt?

They are my children. I am their mother. A mother is supposed to care for her children. I didn't ask for this disease for them. They never asked to be alcoholics. Stop! Please stop! We are not guilty!

I will try hard not to think any more. I will try harder to finish my life with some meaning and fulfillment, in spite of it all. I will not ask why? God, help me. God, help those who suffer loss. God, help the alcoholic. I am not God.

· C H A P T E R 1 7 ·

What we would all like is the happy past restored. Am I
going in circles, or dare I hope I am on a spiral? But if a
spiral, am I going up or down? How often—will it be for
always?

—*C. S. Lewis*
A Grief Observed

I CAN HONESTLY SAY I have not been angry for any real length of time in my whole life. I have seen a lot of angry people, and it has always seemed senseless to me. What good does it do? People who are angry are miserable. They just waste time, their lives. Move on. Forgive, whatever it takes. Forget the anger. It accomplishes nothing.

Everything I have read and experienced says I could be angry. I say, I am not ever angry. Maybe because it is a thing submerged deep within me that is seething. It is simmering, immersed in my being. It is something I know, that with just a little bit of fuel, can explode. An eruption that will decimate everything around me. I will be mad. Insane.

I am angry. I am irritated. I am ready to die or burst. I am mad at everything. I hate what alcohol and drugs have done to my life. My brother, no longer a thriving, living, productive person, succumbed to the demons of liquor and drugs. My son is gone because of the same evil. My daughter hangs in the balance of life and death because of booze. My granddaughter does not have a mother. Everything I love most in the whole damn world has shriveled up and blown away. I am alone in my own private hell if I choose—because of their addictions.

I want to kick things, punch things, and beat on things. Hammer on things. Smash things. I want it to end. I will not be whole until I find a way to peace. I don't know when it will happen or how it will happen. It is all in my pain.

I will still do the best I can each day. I will give myself time. I will realize that all of this is only a part of what has happened in my life. I will go on, in my own time.

I am confused. I will not wonder when the dust will settle on this upheaval of my life. In time I will find peace. I will search for it each day, and it will just happen. Time. There is too much to process now. Time will sort things out. Time will restore me to sanity. Time will bring joy and happiness to my life again. Time is the great healer. It is just what we choose to do with the time. I will take the time I need for time to take its course. Time to reach the next plateau. Time is the key. Oh, God, make the time fly.

I will always have the scars, but I forgive.

CHAPTER 18

I AM THE FIRST to wake. As I climb out of our huge, feather bed, I see Bert. He looks like an angel languishing in the morning light. I dress quietly and start down to the kitchen. As I pass each bedroom, I peek in. Kirk and Janet are sleeping blissfully. During the night, baby Josh somehow made it from his bassinet to now slumber between them. What a handsome grandson I have. Farther down the hall, I peek into Yvette and Brent's room. They are cuddled together like two spoons in a drawer. Another peek into Tony and Julie's room reveals how new their marriage is by the way they have entwined each other. One last peek now before I descend the stairs. I peer into Hope's room to find she is snuggled up in her down comforter. What a precious granddaughter.

I will make breakfast for all of them, and I love it! I will start by grinding fresh coffee beans. I will squeeze just-picked oranges and whip up fluffy buttermilk pancakes with hot maple syrup and freshly churned creamery butter. I will start the bacon last because when everyone smells it frying, they will start descending the stairs. I want to have most of the cooking done so I can enjoy pouring each one of them a steaming cup of coffee. Cooking for them is a labor of love. I have placed clear bowls of water with floating gardenias in the center of our big oak table. Soon they will all be sitting down and munching on everything I have prepared.

My brother and his lovely wife and sweet kids have arrived. Dean is carrying one child under each arm. He extends both children to me for hugs and kisses from Auntie.

Papa and Mama will be bringing their boat by for all of us to go fishing this afternoon. It will be hard to assemble everyone for the outing because after breakfast, the allure of the beach will capture them all. They will want to wander up and down the sandy beach to see what exquisite new shells came to shore last night.

Papa and Mama are here with the boat. We all board and head out to sea. Each of us have turns sitting in the grand fisherman's chair, and we all have a hit of one kind of fish or another. Papa will filet the fish, and Mama will keep them on ice. We will take our catch home for a beach-fire barbecue this evening. Kirk is taking movies of each person as they fish. What an ideal day it is. The ocean is glistening; the sun is warm; the sky is bright blue; and the breeze is cool. Everyone is having a ball!

When we arrive back home, the men head down to the beach to start the fire. Yvette and the girls are busy making au gratin potatoes and tossed salad. I roll all the fish filets in cornmeal, ready to fry. The children cannot wait until we make the s'mores after dinner around the fire. At the close of the meal, Hope will bring her guitar and sing to us. She has a clear, entrancing voice that mists your eyes. She will play songs that we will sing together. We chuckle and taunt those who cannot carry a tune.

Late in the evening we will all go up to the house and get a rousing game of Rummy Royal going. Tony always wins the poker hand, and Bert forgets to pick up the pot when he goes out with the last card played. We roar with laughter, and there are many hugs and kisses. We have such a grand time when we are all together.

The children are getting sleepy, so off to bed they go. Most of us will stay up for hours this evening. There are three full moons tonight. We always watch them till we are blurry-eyed. We sit to-gether on the big cushions on the huge wooden deck overlooking the ocean and marvel at the celestial night sky. There is so much love and happiness encompassing us all. We are so grateful. We are fulfilled. I know I have died and gone to heaven.

CHAPTER 19

YVETTE CALLED. SHE HAS been sober for weeks now. *Thank you, God. Thank you, God. Thank you, God!* I am so grateful. I love you Yvette.

A doctor found an antidepressant that works for her, and she has regained her physical and mental health. *Praise Jesus.*

She said, "Mom, since I lost Hope, I have been in hell for a very long time. Now I am alive." She knows that her panic attacks, anxiety, and severe stressors were being self-medicated with alcohol. At first a way to relax, then a way to cope, then a dependent way to escape. She is eating, exercising, and working. She feels good. She knows that she can live through the horrors that life dishes out with the help of the Lord. She says there will always be stress, but it is part of life.

It is a miracle she is alive. The diabetes alone could have taken her. She knows her diseases up close and personal.

She says she has accepted Kirk's death. She says she knew he would die young.

I'm so sorry Kirk is not here. Maybe in some morbid way he contributes to his sister's sobriety. I know where he is, and that makes me happy. I know that someday he will greet me with open arms.

Tony called. He wants to know if we will be getting together for Easter dinner. He is such a good kid.

I love you, Kirk. I will see you later, standing in the pink clouds.

• CHAPTER 20 •

*Grief and pain are the price we humans have to pay for
the love and total commitment we have for another person.
The more we love, the more we are hurt when we lose the
object of our love. But if we are honest with ourselves would
we have it any other way?*

—C. S. Lewis
A Grief Observed

THERE IS NO WAY to go through life and have it go just the way
we think it should. If life were perfect, we would be in heaven.

Living through conflicts, loss, fear, anger, guilt, and pain is part
of the human condition.

How we choose to live through our life experiences is really up
to each of us. We do find ways to work through all of our trials. Success is linked to the greatest relationship we can have, and that is
with God.

He is here. See how he works in your life. The things he will
bring to your heart, mind, and spirit is not a coincidence. Knowing
him is effortless. He is a loving Father who has huge hands for each
of us to put all of our problems in. We will all go home to be with him
again, from where we came.

So, what did he have in mind for us, to be here on this great
planet earth? Absolutely not to suffer, that is certain. If we search,
we each know that within us is a being who knows truly why we are
here.

The journey does not seem easy, but sometime we do realize it is so simple.

Know that you are a child of God. Life is very harsh without him. When we include him, miracles happen. He proves himself to us every second of our lives. We only need to stop for a while and communicate with him to know how real, loving, and caring he is. He wants us to enjoy this life. He wants us to be happy. He wants us to know that no matter what goes on, he is there to give us what we need. He is an amazing God. I pray you know him.

No matter what life gives us, there is a lot of in-between time. We can make that time good. Please know that most of life is good. Be gentle with yourself. Everything happens as it should.

Today I choose to stand in the pink clouds of God's comfort and peace.

"Blessed are those who mourn, for they will be comforted" (Matthew 5:4).

—Jesus Christ

CPSIA information can be obtained
at www.ICGtesting.com
Printed in the USA
BVHW032149180221
600600BV00007B/83